It's Only Money

Michael Watkins, CFP, FMA, FCSI

It's Only Money

The basics you must know about
planning your personal finances in Canada

Michael Watkins, CFP, FMA, FCSI

2nd Edition 2006

National Library of Canada Cataloguing in Publication

Watkins, Michael, 1971-
It's only money : the basics you must know in planning your finances in Canada / Michael Watkins.

Includes index.
ISBN 0-9734571-0-4

1. Finance, Personal—Canada. I. Title.

HG179.W375 2003 332.024'00971
C2003-907301-7

Cover photo: Denise Pearson
Book design: Jim Bisakowski desktoppublishing@shaw.ca
Printed in Canada

Contents

About the Author

Michael Watkins is a financial planner who identified a need to create a basic yet comprehensive investment guide specifically for Canadians. Michael's professional accreditation includes the Financial Management Advisor (FMA), Certified Financial Planner (CFP) and Fellow of The Canadian Securities Institute (FCSI) designations. He has a bachelor's degree in law from Carleton University in Ottawa and a diploma in Criminology from Mount Royal College in Calgary. His academic distinctions are balanced with real-life experiences as a student, tree planter, security guard, pilot, and banker. Born in Wellington, New Zealand, Michael immigrated to Halifax, Nova Scotia in 1979. He now resides in Mill Bay, British Columbia with his wife Julie and their three children Jordan, Alexandra, and Jenna.

Michael Watkins
(250) 418-0114
mpw1@telus.net

Acknowledgments

There are many individuals I would like to thank for helping me take my ideas and meld them into a book. First, I'd like to thank my wife Julie, my stepchildren Jordan and Alexandra, and my mother Margaret and sister Amanda for their unconditional support and encouragement. I must thank my wife Julie and father Paul as well as Jenny Chomak, who were instrumental in working with me to edit the book as it evolved, and my baby girl Jenna just for being there. Special thanks to Denise Pearson of Imagic Photography for the wonderful cover shot. Thanks to Scot Verleun, Suzanne Rutherford, Matt Varey, Michael Walker, and Jeff Greenburg for their technical support. Rick Montens and Tim Brown of RBS Lawyers, as well as Angus Izard of KPMG ensured that the "i's" were dotted and the "t's" crossed. Finally, thanks to fellow author, Jack Hodgins, for educating me on the ins and outs of getting a book published.

Foreword

It's Only Money

A number of things have become increasingly clear to me about people and money. First, regardless of how much money an individual may have accumulated, most people never seem to feel confident in their ability to live off its proceeds; even if it's in conjunction with a company pension, Canada Pension Plan (CPP), Old Age Security (OAS) or whatever. Second, even though savings are likely to be the number one factor that differentiates a comfortable retirement from a stressful retirement, most people hate to examine their finances and plan for the future.

During my career in the financial services industry, I've had the privilege to work with clients from all levels of income and stages of life. From students to retired professionals, the theme remains constant: Money is something most would like to have, but earning it tends invariably to take precedence over figuring out what to do with it once you have it.

It's not that people don't want to plan for their future or even that they don't know how. It's just that the process seems intangible, long, and boring – the list goes on. Most people would rather volunteer to go to the dentist for a root canal than sit down for however many hours it takes to do their financial plan. Excuses vary: Too busy, uncomfortable with talking about money, don't understand investments, don't want my advisor to think I'm stupid, to name just a few. The reality is that most people spend more time planning their vacation, than planning for their future.

There are tons of books on the subject of money management, so what makes this one any different? This book is intended to be specific to Canadians for a start, and also to be used as a primer. You won't find any complex leveraging schemes designed to melt down your RRSPs in this publication. This book is intended to help you make the most of the money you bring in; not to make you rich. The contents of this book will help you understand the basics of investing and financial planning, but it is still not a replacement for a good financial advisor. In fact, unlike other books on the subject, there is a chapter dedicated to identifying a good financial advisor and establishing a working relationship with your advisor as well as with other experts.

So sit back and relax; the explanations in this book are in plain English and will help take some of the mystery out of financial jargon. By the time you've finished, you should feel confident in your basic knowledge of investing and comfortable that the financial plan you've implemented will guide you to where you want to go, or affirm that you're already on track.

1
The Basics

"I'm so far beyond my income that we may almost be said to be living apart."
e e cummings

Virtually everyone I've ever run into knows the basics of investing. Buy low, sell high, put 10% of your income away every month; you probably know what I'm talking about. And everyone I know would do this if it weren't for two things: Emotions and circumstances. Tune in to the news, read consumer reports or pick up a book, and you are inundated with information to help you become more financially responsible. It would help if you could retain and process all this information like a computer but, unfortunately, few of us can.

We're emotional people. I know, many of you will argue this point and tell me that you think through all of your decisions before making your choices, and maybe you do. However, when we do this, are we making a logical pro and con list, or are we just building logical sounding rationalizations to back up a decision we may have already made? I'll be the first to admit that I belong to the latter group. It's okay though, as long as you're aware of this fact you can work with it.

Asset Allocation

Most advisors subscribe to the investment maxim that 80% to 90% of your overall, long-term investment return is based on the correct mix of '**cash**, **fixed income** and **equity** investments'. There are many other investment approaches, but the asset allocation model works with the average return for each type of investment and over time, regardless of the fund manager involved, most regress to the mean. For example, consider two mutual funds invested in a similar market (e.g. Canadian Equity). In the first year, depending on a number of variables, these two funds may provide drastically different performance results. But as time goes on, the performance edge may see-saw back and forth until the 10 or 20 year averages are only marginally different. This is why the underlying asset class chosen (equities in this case) is more important over the long run than is the selection of a specific fund.

If you've ever sat down with an advisor to make an asset allocation plan, you've probably been questioned about a number of things: When are you going to need this money? What is your **risk tolerance**? How old are you? How much do you make a year? Advisors ask these questions to try and ensure that the recommended investments best fit you as an individual. So far so good. Where we go wrong as investors is that after the plan is completed and the various investments bought, we want to see how good they are. So we watch them. Now you've just told your advisor that it's going to be ten years before you need that money, but darn-it, it has dropped 10% over the last three months! So you go to your advisor with the

Cash (Securities) – Investments with maturities of less than one year. They include short term GICs, Treasury Bills, corporate paper, and bankers acceptances.

Fixed Income (Securities) – Are securities that generate a predetermined periodic interest or dividend income. They include government and corporate bonds, mortgages, and preferred shares.

Equity (Securities) – Shares of stock in a corporation that pay the holder some of the company's profits.

intention to sell out of this bad stock he sold you and buy the stock your neighbour bought which is up 15% in the very same market. This is an emotional reaction.

From your point of view, your reaction is justified; you invested intending to make money - not lose it. Your friend's advisor is obviously much better because he's making money. What we lose sight of here is your time horizon, and the underlying markets that both you and your neighbour are invested in. Remember, you're not alone. I find it painful myself to look at my portfolio during a downturn or **bear market**. It's only the years of education and experience in the field that stop me from selling everything and buying money market funds. So I deal with market downturns by reminding myself that I'm correctly allocated and then largely ignore my portfolio. But I'm getting ahead of myself here. Before we even look at investing, we need to find the money to invest, and that brings us to cash flow.

Cash Flow & Saving Strategies

You know you need to invest, but you can't seem to scrape together the money after your monthly expenses. Most experts advise that you put away an average of 10% of your salary. For a start, this is only a recommendation. If you can only afford to put away 6%, do it. Don't use the fact that you can't find the 10% to invest as an excuse to go shopping. Anything is better than nothing. On the other hand if you can easily afford 20% out of your cash flow, invest the most you can without making yourself short on cash. Many of my clients who have cash flow issues have large salaries, but also tend to spend accordingly. So if you have an inflow of money greater than your needs, put it

Risk Tolerance - The financial and psychological readiness of an individual to bear the day-to-day fluctuations in the value of their investments. People who are unable to tolerate risk are said to be risk averse. Those who like to take risk are risk loving.

Bear Market - A situation in a stock or commodity market in which stockholders are selling in anticipation of falling prices.

away before temptation gets the better of you. Now that doesn't necessarily mean you have to lock it up in your retirement portfolio. These days an emergency fund is also a necessity.

Every day we're bombarded by advertising designed to make us feel that we simply *must* have three TVs, two nice cars and a Harley for the weekends. It's no wonder Canadians spend to the maximum extent of their cash flow, regardless of income. And when we haven't got cash, plastic is just as good. We've become addicted to borrowing. The old method of saving up to buy that suit you really wanted is virtually extinct. Now I know not everyone owes money, but most of us do. In the last 15 years, Statistics Canada has seen our consumer debt more than *double* while our savings rate has virtually fallen off the chart. We're better at saving than Americans, but just marginally. This trend is reversible once it's recognized for what it is. You don't necessarily have to have an ironclad budget for every little thing you spend in a week, but you should be able to exert some control over your spending.

Money Market Fund – These are considered to be the lowest risk of all mutual fund investments. The fund invests in money market securities, such as T-Bills and commercial paper.

GICs – Guaranteed Investment Certificates are essentially interest bearing loans made to a bank or trust company for a specified term for a specified annual interest rate. Secure, because they are insured by the Canadian Deposit Insurance Corporation for up to $60,000.

Loads – A charge that is added to the price of some mutual fund shares as a commission or marketing cost.

Consolidation Loans – A loan for the purpose of consolidating all of one's debt in one product for lower interest rates and ease of re-payment.

There are several ways to get out of the credit crunch, but start by paying yourself first. This advice is always number one on the list for a reason: *It works*. People tend to spend what they have in the bank, so if you have automatic debits going into an investment account, the temptation, as well as the ability to spend your money, is greatly reduced. As a further bit of advice, use an investment vehicle that's not readily accessible. A simple savings account may be easy to put money into, but it's just too easy to get it back out. You can always put more in next payday, right? No. Use a **money market** account. Yes, it's a mutual fund, but it's a very stable one and tends to give you the best return on short-term cash without the constraints attached to most cashable **GICs**. It also normally takes 24 hours to get the money out, so there's a built-in cooling off period between seeing the Big Bula Driver with the titanium shaft and having the ability to pay for it.

A quick note on money market funds; they're very simple, so the MERs, or Management Expense Ratios (read service charges), should be lower than other mutual funds. Also, never purchase a money market fund from a company that charges commissions or loads on them, as they all perform very closely and there are ample money market funds without **loads**. While we're on the subject, a load is an additional charge placed either on the purchase or the redemption of a mutual fund.

Gain Control of Your Spending Habits

One of the best ways to gain control of your spending habits is to audit yourself. You need to know where your money is going. It's best to use a pay period rather than just a week since people's spending habits tend to vary significantly during the time between paychecks, so picking a week at random may not work. For example, let's say you get paid every two weeks. The first week after getting paid may be taken up with paying all the bills and catching up on shopping, while the week after may be absolutely quiet of the spending front. To be really thorough, the best audit would be a month, although it may be unrealistic for most people to have the time to focus on that kind of project for that length of time.

Once you've determined when and how you're going to do the audit, buy yourself a cheap notebook and spend the designated period of time writing down every single thing you spend money on, and I mean everything – car payments, mortgage, dinner out; everything down to your last cup of coffee. At the end of this period, total up all of your expenses and make two categories, "essential" and "luxury". And no, a double shot of espresso in the morning is not truly a necessity. Look for any red flags that pop up. If you're spending an average of $10 a day on luxuries, perhaps that's an area to cut back on. $10 a day is $3,650 a year. Put that away in long-term investments and pretty soon we're talking real money.

Another way to gain control of your spending is to set limits. If you find yourself making impulse buys, you might want to start placing an automatic hold on any purchase over $100 for example. So, if you're out shopping and you see something you really want, ask the clerk to put it aside and then wait for a couple of days before buying it. This cooling off period may allow you time to see if you really need the item, or if it's just an impulse buy.

Debt Reduction Strategies

Consolidate your debt: Some people associate **consolidation loans** with bad credit, but this simply isn't true. If you decide to clean up your borrowing, a consolidation loan is the way to go. Credit card companies can charge anywhere between 10% to 30% on their lending products. Your bank may provide a consolidation loan at only 2% over the prime lending rate providing you're a loyal client with a decent credit rating. If you use collateral, that rate can drop even further.

Now I don't want everyone running to the bank and saying I said they could have a loan at Prime +2. Lending is an exercise in risk management. If you have a good credit history, you get preferential rates. However, if you've been remiss in paying off your debts in a timely fashion, the banks will charge you a higher rate of interest (to offset the risk that you might default on the loan). Don't take offense to this; it's not personal and, in most cases, even if the rate for your consolidation loan is more than Prime +2, it's still much better than that offered by your various credit card companies.

Once you've consolidated your debt, *cut up all your credit cards except one*. Be forewarned, as you'll be inundated with offers of new cards in the future, but remain strong; all you really need is one.

I do recommend keeping one credit card, because more and more companies use credit cards to secure seat reservations, hotel rooms, etc.

If it turns out that you can't get a consolidation loan, don't get in a funk and give up, instead attack your debt systematically. Focus on eliminating *one debt at a time* starting with the most expensive, that is the one with the *highest interest rate*. Pay the bare minimum on all of your other debts until the most expensive is eliminated, then move down to the next one on your list.

Finally, lets have a closer look at those people out there who we're trying to keep up with. If you've seen someone making a large purchase, such as a Porsche, put it in perspective. If you're aware that their income is significantly higher than yours do the math. For them, buying that Porsche may be equivalent to you picking up a 1990 Chevy Cavalier. If they make the same as you and still bought a Porsche, console yourself with the knowledge that they may have to sell it in a few months to pay for groceries.

So after a couple of months, you've got your debt under control and you're putting money away automatically on each paycheque; this is an excellent position to be in. But now you must determine how to allocate your investment resources and invest the money you've saved. You'll need to address your emergency fund as well as plan for retirement, your children's education, and any other specific goals you may have. But before we attack your goals, and planning in general, we need to look at your options for investing in Canada.

2
Investing

"Wealth is not without its advantages, and the case to the contrary, although it has often been made, has never proved widely persuasive."

– John Kenneth Galbraith

Investment Types

Of the multitude of investment options available to Canadians, regardless of what you choose, it will fall into one of three basic types: cash, fixed income, and equities.

Cash securities are basically any investment than can be converted to cash in less than one year. Money market, treasury bills and GICs of a year or less are all examples. Generally, you'll want to include these as a small part of your overall portfolio, as cash has in fact been the top performing asset class in several years past and allows for some liquidity. Also, you may want to invest in cash for emergency funds or very short-term investments, as the volatility is very low.

Fixed income securities are investments that generate predetermined periodic interest or dividend income. In other words, when you purchase a fixed income investment, you can be confident in the rate of return as long as you hold the product to its maturity. Having said that, these investments can be traded prior to maturity for greater or lesser than their face value depending on market conditions. GICs with maturities greater than one year, bonds, mortgages, and preferred shares are examples of this type of security. To clarify;

preferred shares are included in fixed income, because unlike common shares, the preferred dividend rate is fixed regardless of the profitability of the underlying company.

Equities are investments designed to create dividend income and capital gains. Common shares of publicly traded companies are the prevalent investments in this type of security.

Time-in and Timing the Market

Regardless of what you invest in, time is your best friend. The more time you have to invest, the greater your potential overall return. If you have a longer time horizon, you can afford to take on more risk or **volatility** simply because you can ride out any significant downturns in the market.

Investment growth increases with each year you stay invested, so taking your money out of the market during a downturn may save you from short-term losses, but has two consequences. First, you're losing valuable time in the market. Second, you stand a better than average chance of missing the best two or three days of the imminent market upswing. By nature, people wait to see the positive market turn before they get back in, and so miss out on what can be half the returns for the year. It all comes back to emotions. The best time to buy often seems the worst, and the worst time to sell often looks to be the best answer at the time. So staying invested with a disciplined, diversified portfolio is the best strategy.

Volatility – Measures the periodic change in returns in relation to the average or mean return – the greater the change, the more volatile the investment. A volatile investment is a risky investment.

Accurately predicting when the markets have hit their floor and start to swing back up is extremely difficult, if not impossible. Since 1960 and including the current market, the TSE 300 (Toronto Stock Exchange) has seen a total of eight corrections of varying degrees and duration. Prior to the turn of the millennium, the longest correction began in May of 1965 and lasted for 16 months with a total loss of approximately 12%. The shortest was only six months beginning in May of 1998 but was much more severe with a 26% loss. No one can see into the future, but experience has taught us that selling in a down market to avoid further loss merely crystallizes the paper losses you see and along with that comes the chance of missing the initial, and often strongest, days of the upswing.

Markets do eventually bounce back and often in a much shorter period than we experienced in 2000. But rather than trying to time the market for your investment purchases, making regular contributions removes all the guesswork, and a lot of the risk. Be it weekly, biweekly, semi-monthly, or monthly; regular investing has a number of important benefits.

Dollar Cost Averaging

Considering what we know about budgeting, most of us would agree it's usually much easier to find the money for a weekly contribution than it is to gather a proportionate amount for an annual contribution. This also works with the spending theory of "out of sight, out of mind" to help you resist the urge to splurge. But if you only make investment purchases annually, you're at the mercy of the market. It is possible that you may be perfectly positioned to take maximum advantage of the market, but it's statistically much more likely that you've missed the boat. Not to mention that making smaller contributions throughout the year gives you longer time in the market than waiting until the end of the year to scrape together a contribution.

This concept, called dollar cost averaging, works on the premise that up or down, by investing at regular intervals, you're going to average a higher return over the long run than by trying to guess what the market is going to do next and then investing. The big secret here is that massive investment firms pay millions of dollars to their economists and research analysts every year and they're still wrong half the time.

Market watching can be addictive, especially in a world that now has CNN and CNBC going 24/7. It's true that information is power, but too much information can stress you out and can cause you to take action at a point that is, most likely, precisely the wrong time. Networks and newspapers want to make the news interesting so they tend to emphasize market swings and events, overanalyzing them to create viewer and reader interest.

My advice to my clients during a rough market is to review the planning that went into their portfolio selection. If nothing has changed in their goals and circumstances, then the best course of action is to stay invested, and ignore your portfolio statements and the news. Making *short-term* decisions and applying them to your *long-term* plan is generally not a wise decision. While no one enjoys going through a market downturn, investors should understand that it is completely normal for the **equity markets** to fluctuate and occasionally post negative returns. Think of the market as a guy with a yo-yo walking up some stairs. You can either focus on the yo-yo or the progress up the stairs. Investors uncomfortable with this might want to re-evaluate their personal tolerance for risk. If you're not sleeping at night, even if your portfolio is making you money, perhaps you need to be a little more conservative.

Market fluctuations are a certainty, and the nature of investing is the rise and fall of share value. It would be more unusual if stock values *didn't* change. History shows us again and again that remaining invested is the best way to withstand short-term market volatility and build long-term wealth.

Equity Market – An organized market where brokers meet to buy and sell stocks and shares.

Performance & Volatility

While we're on the topic of market performance, there are some amazingly effective commercials in the papers and on TV these days that show people obviously very comfortable in their retirement. The gist of these commercials is basically the same: Come invest with us, and we'll ensure the kind of retirement you deserve. The really good ads never flat out say how, and the reason is fairly simple. Most investment companies use very similar models for diversification of investments and estimating returns, but they have to differentiate themselves from the pack. Some may be able to say that they have the best-educated or most experienced advisors, but that doesn't sell funds.

> Annualized – To calculate or adjust figures so that they reflect a period of a year.

What does sell is performance. Open any newspaper and turn to the financial section. You'll see several ads giving you hard data on the performance of their funds over the last year, three years, five, etc. Note that these return percentages are **annualized** (which tends to hide volatility rather well) and are persuasive. Investors look at these numbers and say, "Wow! XYZ Techno fund just got a return of 356% over the last year and has average 45% over the last five! That's awesome! I want to get in on that." The fact that XYZ Techno fund actually lost 50% last year is glossed over by the annualized numbers. Furthermore, with some minor exceptions, you never see the same funds advertised repeatedly. This is because specific funds inevitably fall off the high-performance pedestal or suffer as the market favours a completely different investment style. So in an equity market slump, fund companies dust off their fixed income funds and point out that while everyone else's investment portfolios are crashing, we've got a bond fund that picked up 10% this year!

So it's no surprise that investors chase performance. However, there are a number of problems with this approach. First of all, by the time these amazing returns hit the papers, the fund or market has already peaked or will peak shortly. So you're buying high. Second, it has been proven that while many fund managers are able to beat the benchmarks for one year, the numbers who continue to beat the mark drops off sharply with each subsequent year. A study by the Financial Resource Corporation of Boston found that investors who bought on past performance *averaged 20% lower returns over three year holding periods between 1990 and 2000.*

So, is performance still important? Sure it is, but not in the superstar kind of way. What you want to look for in an investment portfolio is strong overall performance with some consistency. As I said before, no one beats the benchmark all the time. What you want are funds or fund managers that are consistently in the top two quartiles with lower volatility than their peers. You may have heard of quartile rankings before, but just to clarify: A 1st quartile fund is in the top 25% of its fund peers (funds with the same basic mandate, e.g. Canadian Equity); A 2nd quartile fund is in the top 50% of its peers; A 3rd quartile fund is in the bottom 50%; and, A 4th quartile fund lurks in the basement.

You should try and build your portfolio with funds that have longer-term returns in the top two quartiles. Don't throw out a fund that had one bad year if the rest looked good. All it takes is a couple of bad picks or missed opportunities by a fund manager in a year to make the difference between 2nd and 3rd quartile in the rankings. More attention should be paid to the manager's consistency and the fund's historical volatility.

The best way to think about your portfolio is as a team. This approach lets you view your funds as individuals who play different roles, but come together as a whole that is greater than the sum of its parts. A mortgage fund may have been a drag on your portfolio for a few years, but it may have propped up the portfolio when the equity markets crashed. This goes back to the diversification approach and is precisely the reason we don't put all our money in one basket.

I'm always hearing from clients who want to drop their "dogs". You know, a fund that may be returning far less than the other funds in their portfolio. This may be because it is an under performing investment, or it may just be that its asset class isn't the leading performer this year. With regard to long-term performance and reduced volatility, a good team of funds beats an individual superstar any day. It's fun to be on the hockey team that has the league scoring leader on it, but its even better to be on the team that wins the Stanley Cup.

Risk

Investing often comes down to an exercise in risk and return. The basic rule of thumb is that the greater the return you seek to gain, the greater amount of risk you will need to take on. This is accurate for not only different types of investments, but also the same investments offered by different institutions. It's pretty obvious that shooting for a 10% return in the stock market is a little riskier than looking for 4% from a GIC. What is a little less obvious is that choosing a similar GIC at 5% offered by a competing institution also exposes you to more risk, if only marginally so.

It may seem that a GIC is a GIC and the Canadian Deposit Insurance Corporation (CDIC) covers them all. However, the institution that's offering a premium rate (possibly over their breakeven point) is likely cash poor, and needs an inflow of cash to fund their lending book. This often results in too much cash; which they then offset by dropping rates. Smaller institutions do this all the time, as they don't have the massive, stabilizing customer base of the big banks. It can certainly be advantageous to the consumer, as long as this see-saw doesn't get out of hand and these **loss leaders** don't cut too deeply into the institutions cash flow, causing insolvency in the institution.

When most people think of risk as it relates to investing, the first image that comes to mind may be gambling on some hot stock tip that they heard from a friend. As such, mention the word mutual funds to a conservative investor and they'll think of stock markets and risk. The perception of investing that many people have is that stocks are risky and bonds are safe. This is both right and wrong.

First of all, let me emphasize that the risk I was just talking about is market risk. Just one of the many types of risk you can get into when investing. I'm not going to go over all the risk forms, but I will highlight a few of the main ones and explain the differences.

Market risk refers to the volatility an investor may experience while being invested. The image

Loss Leaders – An item sold at a price below its cost in the hope that customers who buy it will also buy other products.

this creates is of wildly fluctuating stock markets, but this is not the whole picture. Yes stocks do go up and down, but so do bond prices and yields. The common perception that bonds are less risky than stocks depends completely on which stocks and bonds you're talking about. For instance, two identically priced stocks may have completely different performance profiles.

A highflying tech stock on the NASDAQ exchange may experience far more volatility than a blue chip stock on the New York Stock Exchange (NYSE). So far, no surprises, so let's jump to bonds for a moment. Bonds have a maturity date and if purchased at their initial sale date and held to maturity, any volatility that the value of the bond experiences during its lifecycle can largely be ignored. It's when you want to sell a bond prior to maturity or purchase a bond after its initial offering that market value comes into play.

Bonds also come in many shapes and sizes. For example, government and corporate bonds can be rated from AAA to junk. The volatility associated with a AAA bond would be much less than that of a junk bond. However, the possibility of default is still there and increases as the bond rating goes down. Now if we compare the stocks and bonds I just mentioned; the junk bond is likely to be more volatile than the blue chip stock, so demonstrating that stocks and bonds do not necessarily have distinct levels of risk in and of themselves, but can be just as volatile as each other.

Now a number of you are no doubt thinking that at this point you'll just ignore the whole mess and stick to GICs. Granted that would effectively eliminate market risk, but would also open you up to a couple of other forms of risk, namely interest rate risk and purchasing power risk through inflation.

Interest rate risk is the risk that when your GIC matures, the prevailing rate will be lower than it was at the time you originally purchased the GIC. A lot of my clients who had money in the 1980s harken back fondly to a time when they could buy an 18% GIC. Obviously rates have dropped significantly since then and this is interest rate risk. Inflationary risk (also known as purchasing power risk) goes hand in hand with interest rates. Looking at the 1980s again, while you were earning double-digit returns on your GICs, chances are you weren't beating inflation.

Inflation is the increase in the cost of goods and living expenses. So lets say you made 15% on your investments in an 18% inflationary period. You would actually be losing 3% in purchasing power. That's inflationary risk.

Foreign exchange risk is an issue that became more apparent when the Canadian dollar experienced rapid weakening against the U.S. dollar. If you chose to sock money into U.S. investments while our dollar declined, you would experience a foreign exchange loss if and when the Canadian dollar strengthened.

Think about it this way. You decide to move to the United States for six months for a business opportunity and set aside $10,000 Canadian to buy a car to drive around while you're down there. The exchange rate is 65 cents U.S. which gives you $6,500 U.S.. Meanwhile, while you're away, the value of the Canadian dollar goes up relative to the American dollar, and the exchange rate becomes 70 cents U.S.. You decide to sell the car in the States rather than bring it back to Canada, and you even manage to sell it for the same price you bought it, $6,500 U.S.. However, because of the rise in the Canadian dollar, once you exchange your money back to Canadian, you walk away with $9,285 in your pocket. Apply this to investing in foreign investments, remembering that the value of the Canadian dollar moves constantly, and you can appreciate foreign exchange risk. It's the risk that the value of an investment denominated in foreign currencies will fall if the foreign exchange rate of a domestic currency rises.

Several other forms of risk are liquidity, time, and default. As you might guess, liquidity risk refers to the chance that an investment holder will have difficulty finding a buyer for the investments they're currently holding. Think of Bre-X, the huge goldmine scandal of the late 1990s. During their peak, liquidity of the shares was not a problem, but as the scandal progressed and market value plummeted, shareholders were finding it more and more difficult to unload their stock, even at bargain basement prices. By the time the crash had finished, entrepreneurial shareholders were selling their stock certificates on the streets as souvenirs.

Time risk refers to the uncertainty about future events that an investor accepts by promising to hold an investment for a defined length of time.

Default risk refers to the chance that an issuer of a bond will not be able to repay the loan or that the company whose stock is purchased will not be profitable.

Finally, I'd like to discuss systemic risk versus un-systemic risk. These two risk factors are more broad based and actually very important to understanding risk as a whole. Systemic risk refers to factors that have a blanket effect over the market as a whole, while un-systemic risk can affect an individual security without necessarily affecting all securities. The tragedy of September 11th is a perfect example of systemic risk. Not specific to any one market sector or stock (although it did affect certain industries like travel and tourism far more than others), this event had the effect of pushing out the projected recovery of the market by several months.

Generally, un-systemic risk is associated with the type of business and the financial situation of the underlying company. The energy situation in some of the American states provides a good example of un-systemic risk. In the past, energy price regulations combined with soaring production costs crippled energy providers in California, resulting in rolling blackouts as the companies made a desperate bid to remain solvent. Clearly, this had an adverse effect on their share prices.

It's fair to say that no investment is completely risk free. As you can see, there are many more forms of risk working on your investment portfolio than perhaps you may have been previously aware of. Every form of investment has one or more forms of risk associated with it. This is not meant to discourage you from investing, but rather to help you understand the risks that are out there.

In the past many of my clients shied away from mutual funds because of a perception of risk. However, investors discovered that they were encountering more risk by holding a portfolio solely made up of GICs, rather than if they had been invested in a well diversified portfolio. To close out this section on risk, I'd like to discuss a different emotional reaction to market volatility.

We've all heard the expression "once bitten, twice shy", and certainly in the wake of September 11th and the Enron crisis we saw a lot of investors shy away from the market. But not all investors behave this way. Often, investors whose portfolios have been damaged by market volatility, respond by taking on more risk in an effort to quickly restore their portfolios to their former status. The mindset here is much like that of a gambler who loses a hand then doubles his bet on the next hand to make back his loss, hoping that his luck will improve and lightning won't strike twice. As you can see, this is an emotional response that can again be overcome by a disciplined investing strategy.

I know that in the wake of a major market downturn it can be very difficult to see the light at the end of the tunnel, but it's there. If your portfolio is established properly, you're diversified and making regular contributions, you have nothing to fear; time will heal your portfolio. However, if you were grossly overexposed by shifting your portfolio to take advantage of a "sure thing" and then the market crashed, making another gamble will only increase your woes.

Diversification & Mutual Funds

These days, more and more investors are turning to mutual funds for instant diversification. These funds have become almost synonymous with investing in the Canadian landscape. Why is this? What exactly is a mutual fund, and how did they become so popular? In the greater scheme of investing over history, mutual funds are a relatively new option in a vast array of choices offered to the modern investor.

We can see the precursor to the mutual fund, if we look back to the **fixed trust** of the mid-nineteenth century. These trusts were set up to hold domestic and foreign government bonds. Once created, no changes were made to the trusts, so there was no management per se. Because of that, once the bonds it held had matured, the trust dissolved, and paid out to the investor. This was certainly a viable investment vehicle for its time, but it lacked flexibility and diversification, so a new product offering was born with the closed-end fund.

England pioneered these funds in the early twentieth century. Simply put, these funds were corporations in the business of investing. The corporation exchanged shares for investment capital and then used the funds raised to make investments of their own. Income generated by the company was then distributed back to the shareholders. Closed-end funds are very similar to mutual funds, with one major difference. Closed-end funds trade on the open market or stock exchanges, and their value is determined by market demand for the fund's shares, which is indirectly impacted by the fund's underlying holdings. This contrasts sharply with the mutual fund, whose units are traded directly with the *mutual fund itself* instead of the open market. As such, the value of the fund is derived directly from the market value of its *underlying securities*.

Fixed Trust – An unmanaged pool of debt securities that all mature at the same time. The pool is created by an investment dealer who then sells units of the pool to investors. Unlike a bond fund, a fixed trust has a limited life.

As with investments in general, the types of mutual funds available vary greatly, as does the risk associated with each one. There are currently over 4,000 different mutual funds available for purchase in Canada alone; all of which will fall into one of four basic categories.

Money market funds represent the lowest risk of all mutual funds. Holdings may include a mix of short-term T-Bills, GICs, commercial paper and bankers' acceptances. In a well-diversified portfolio, money market type funds are used to serve as a source of ready cash to make additional fund purchases, and provide a solid base in the rare occurrence that cash is the highest performing asset class of the time.

Fixed income funds are often considered the next level of risk in mutual funds. Certainly, the volatility associated with these funds is not as great as some of the more aggressive equity funds, but that doesn't mean they are without risk. These funds invest primarily in longer-term bonds, mortgages and preferred shares, and these investments tend to react inversely to equity market fluctuations. The main purpose of fixed income funds is, as the name implies, to generate an income stream at a greater average rate of return than money market funds.

Balanced funds bridge the gap between fixed income and equity funds, essentially forming mini portfolios within your overall portfolio of funds. These funds have varying mixes of investments in accordance to their stated goals, which are rebalanced by the fund manager to take advantage of market conditions. Generally, these funds are used as a building block to grow your portfolio to a certain size before further diversifying into various cash, fixed income and equity funds.

Equity funds invest primarily in common shares of publicly traded companies. Depending on their mandate, these funds can be extremely speculative or relatively stable and can run the gamut from extremely specialized to very broad based. International equity funds hold similar investments, but with a focus on foreign companies. These funds may take a worldwide approach, or even focus on one specific country.

Fees & Commissions

Regardless of the type of fund, they all share a common feature in that all are subject to **Management Expense Ratios (MERs)**. If you wanted to put a price tag on a mutual fund, this would be it. MERs are simply the expense incurred by a particular mutual fund as its management team engages in investment trading, analysis and administration. This cost is *taken off the top of whatever return the fund produces in a given year*. So, if your fund returned 8% and it has an MER of 2%, it

Management Expense Ratios (MERs) – A calculation that is required under National Policy 39. It allows investors to compare the level of management fees and expenses from one fund to another.

actually grew by 10% during that year. This may not seem like a big deal if you're getting double-digit returns, but becomes significantly more important during market slumps and single digit performance. The MER is *taken regardless of performance*, so even if your fund is losing money, the fees come off.

MERs aren't the only thing you should look at when considering a fund, but they should be given serious consideration. Generally, as the cost and complexity of managing a fund increases, so too does the MER associated with it. So a low volatility, low turnover fund like a money market fund, should have an MER closer to 1%, while a foreign equity fund may be approaching 3%. You can't negotiate or eliminate MERs, but fund loads (or service fees) are another matter.

Loads, service fees, sales charges: They are all essentially the same thing. They are negotiable charges that are set up to pay for the advisor's ongoing advice and service, and they are charged over and above the MER. A load may be charged either at the time the units are bought, or at the time units are sold. The amount is based on a specific percentage of the dollar amount of the units that were bought or sold. To further clarify the differences between loads and MERs, think of who gets paid. The MER is unavoidable because it is the money that helps to pay for all of the research and management costs that go into the fund itself. In other words, the MER pays for the fund manager's salary, data analysis, etc. The load on the other hand, goes to pay for the distribution channels. So it's better to think of it as a commission paid to the sales force.

Depending on where you buy your investments, you may be offered the choice of front-end, deferred, or no sales charge on the mutual fund purchase. At first glance, you might say that obviously the no-charge (or no-load) funds would be the way to go; and most Canadian banking institutions offer no-load funds as part of their investment line-up. However, always keep in the back of your mind that age old sentiment that "there's no such thing as a free ride". No-load funds may actually have the purchase cost built into the MER or, in the case of the major Canadian banks, you're paying the advisor's salary through a combination of the profit from the funds, GICs, lending, etc.

If the sales fee is applied at the time of purchase, it's known as a front-end load and is based on the total dollar amount invested to purchase the units of the mutual fund. A load is designed to compensate the advisor for his or her advice and can range anywhere from 0% to 9%, but by law can reach as high as 12%. Often this charge is open for negotiation.

No-loaded – A mutual fund that does not charge an additional fee, or load, is termed unloaded.

So what's better: No-load, deferred or front-end charge funds? As usual, there's no easy answer. Each is useful depending on what you need your money to do. Obviously, if you just have a short-term cash need, a no-load money market fund may be the most suitable. But let's look at front-end versus back-end loaded funds over the long term. Depending on the negotiated front-end load, it may be more cost-effective to buy a front-end fund if you are going to start generating an income stream and drawing from the fund right away. This is because the deferred charges of a back-end load fund may be higher than the front-end cost in the beginning. However, if you plan on investing for the long term without the need to draw on your funds in the short term, deferred charge funds may be the way to go. To further complicate matters, many front-end load funds actually have *reduced* MERs versus the identical back-ended fund. In this case, ask your advisor to do a future value calculation on the growth of the investment using front and back-end MERs to determine the best choice.

Real Estate as an Investment

Over the last couple of years, more and more people have been turning to real estate as an alternative to stocks, bonds and mutual funds for investing their money. It's easy to see why: After the dot-com bubble burst in early 2000, the investment market has been fairly volatile. People that had sold out of their investments began to look around for alternatives and quickly realized that their homes had averaged a solid growth in value of between 4% to 6% on average over the last fourty years. In addition, these "real estate investments" were tactile: something that could be seen, touched and improved on; while stocks, bonds and mutual funds were merely pieces of paper or numbers on a financial statement.

To make real estate even more attractive, the Government began rapidly lowering interest rates to stimulate the faltering economy, making it easier to afford a home. These factors, along with a number of others, created a bull market for real estate and, consequently, people have experienced extremely high growth rates in property over the last couple of years. So, the question that many are beginning to ask is this, "Will real estate continue its rapid growth, or is it just another bubble"?

The answer lies somewhere in between. With the Government raising interest rates and the real estate market becoming over-saturated with product, demand will most likely begin to fall. This, however, will likely not cause a massive crash in real estate prices like we saw with the tech implosion. Most likely there will be a gradual decline in growth rates to a possible flattening of the market or perhaps even a slight decline in value on average over the short term. However, certain real estate markets that experienced truly exceptional growth rates over the last few years may feel a stronger retraction.

I view real estate as merely another viable investment. Just like stocks, bonds and mutual funds, real estate is going to have its major surges, its retractions and its flat periods. And just like any other investment, trying to time a real estate purchase to get-in and get-out for a quick buck is a dangerous game. Investing can be counter-intuitive in that when any market, be it real estate or otherwise, looks its best the peak has probably already passed. When things look the bleakest, that is in fact the best time to buy. But how do you really know? No-one has a crystal ball, so that's why I advise my clients to diversify and stay disciplined in their investing strategy. Real estate has a definite place in your portfolio, just keep it in perspective.

Common Investing Errors

There are a ton of mistakes you can make while trying to make the right investment decisions. Probably the most prevalent, and best highlighted by the late 1990s bull market, is an aversion to selling your winners. Investors often make very rational and good choices in making an investment purchase, whether it is a stock, bond, fund, or whatever. However, in a bull market the problem lies not in an investment's lack of performance, but in its over-performance. Too often as an advisor, I am told by my clients that they are only going to hold the fund/stock just a little longer, say when it hits $100 a share. Waiting for a magic number or a round figure is often a mistake. But as we saw in 2001, when a market falls, it can happen quickly and unexpectedly. This, of course, leads to another common problem: Not wanting to sell a declining stock for fear of missing the up-tick.

This may come as a surprise to some, but many clients are extremely reluctant to sell a losing investment. Coined "the endowment effect". It results from investors mentally perceiving a greater value in the investment because of their ownership, and it can restrict them from making a more rational decision to walk away from it. People are by nature quite loyal, and this transfers easily to the companies that they invest in. The best examples I can think of are the share purchase programs that many companies offer as a benefit to their employees.

Often, employees can amass large amounts of stock without realizing it, and become reluctant to sell out of loyalty to the company or the perception that they know a lot about the corporation. The fall of Enron in the United States is a perfect example of the pitfalls of this practice. Discipline and diversification still need to be applied, even if it means not making as much in another stock or form of investment. The downside of amassing the majority of your investment portfolio in one stock can be catastrophic.

A strategy many of my clients choose to follow is to set a target that they'd like to reach from the start, and then average out of the stock in smaller chunks after they reach that target. This helps take the emotions and guesswork out of the equation. Sometimes the stock just keeps going up, which can be difficult to watch from the sidelines, but often a serious loss is avoided. Either way, you've achieved your target. Also, set a level at which you will sell the investment if it free falls. As with anything in life, if you have an intelligently crafted plan in place, your successes will outweigh your failures.

Now it may come as a bit of a surprise to some (particularly men) but, as a whole, women investors tend to outperform their male counterparts. Nine out of the last twelve years, investment groups consisting of women only have outperformed the male only groups on the basis of net return on investment. It's significant to note that the margin of victory wasn't exactly slim. For example, the National Association of Investors in the U.S. studied investment clubs and determined that in 1996, the "women only" clubs averaged a 21% return while the "men only" picked up 15%.

Studies have determined the reason for this disparity comes down to discipline. Men as a group tend to trade more often, looking for trends and hot market segments, usually to their detriment. However, women as a group typically build an investment plan and stick to it; thus reducing their transactional costs and avoiding the buy high, sell low problem.

So after implementing and sticking to your strategy, you make some serious profits. But now you've made so much money you're afraid you'll take a tax hit of up to 25%. No one wants to give the government more than their share, but why sit on an investment risking a 40% or 50% market drop over paying taxes on your profits? Many of my clients have complained to me that they don't want to sell their high performing investment because of the tax hit. So is it better to wait for the investment to start losing money so you don't have to pay any taxes? Of course not. You have to go into investing with the knowledge that you have to pay taxes on your profit.

Emergency Funds

Most often we associate investing with either a short or long-term goal. However, we also need to be prepared for the unexpected: Enter the emergency fund. The use of an emergency fund is a theory that's been around in financial planning circles for a long time. These days, an emergency fund of some form is an absolute necessity, and the rule of thumb is generally three to six months wages.

Over 1 million workers in the U.S. and Canada were laid off in 2001. Salaries have been frozen and bonuses are down significantly. This economic reality, combined with the likelihood of experiencing a major home or vehicle repair, family crisis or becoming disabled or getting laid off, and it becomes apparent that without being prepared, you might have to dip into your retirement savings.

If your savings are non-registered, you may have to sell out of some investments at a less than opportune time in the market cycle. While this may be bad enough, it's not as bad as it could be. If all of your savings are tied up in RRSPs, you may experience the previous problem as well as risk a nasty tax snowball effect depending on the extent to which you need to redeem your RRSPs.

When you make a redemption from RRSPs in a lump sum, a number of things happen. First of all, you lose that **contribution room** (unless you're drawing out under the First Time Homebuyers or Lifelong Leaning Plans) and you can never get it back. Second, all of the money drawn from the plan is added to your income for that year. Depending on what your income is normally, that can catapult you quickly into the next tax bracket. I've heard horror stories of clients drawing on their RRSPs to pay taxes, only to be taxed again

Contribution Room – Anyone with earned income for RRSP purposes or certain other types of income can invest in RRSPs up to the end of the year they reach 69. Currently, the amount of contribution an individual has is determined by multiplying his or her earned income by 18% to a maximum of $14,500 (soon to increase) plus any room carried forward from previous years less the Pension Adjustment.

in the next tax year on the income created by the RRSP redemption. The key to determining your needs for an emergency fund is to visualize the worst financial situation that you can get into and prepare for it accordingly.

An issue relating to being laid off that needs to be addressed is consideration regarding the package or buy-out you may receive from your company. Canada Customs and Revenue Agency (CCRA) applies a formula that restricts the amount of your package that is eligible for RRSP contribution based on your length of employment. The amount that can be transferred to your RRSP is $2,000 for each calendar year (or part year) of service before 1996, plus $1,500 for each year (or part year) before 1989 for which employer contributions to your pension plan have not **vested**.

> Vested – Having an unquestionable right to the possession of property or privilege. In this case, the pension contributions made by your employer are usually held to be non-vested until a specific period of time has passed, after which they become your property.

Having said that, if you still have previously accumulated RRSP room available, nothing prevents you from using that room to shelter the ineligible portion of your package. So you may be forced to declare a very large increase in your income for that year which will most likely catapult you into the maximum tax bracket if you're not already there. If you receive your package in a year after the year you terminated employment, it may be more advantageous to have the CCRA recalculate the tax on the income as if you received it in the previous year to which the payment relates. This option may relieve the higher tax liability that would result if the entire lump sum were taxed in the year of receipt.

Investment Fraud and Scams

Every once in a while, one of my clients calls me or drops by with an email they've received showing them how to make huge amounts of money in a no-risk investment scheme. It invariably turns out to be a scam of some kind, or the risks involved are far greater than the advertisement would have you believe. Scams and investment fraud has been around a long time, however with the advent of the internet and email, it's becoming more frequent and happening to more and more people. I wanted to add a few points to help people recognize them for what they are, so I've listed them below.

1) **Sky high returns**: Risk and return is generally directly related. Anytime you hear of a return that sounds too good to be true, be sure to do your homework. You need to understand the risks involved and it never hurts to get a second opinion.
2) **Absolutely no risk**: Goes hand in hand with the previous point. Every investment has risks, even GICs. Make sure you understand the investment and know the risks associated with it. Always diversify your investments.
3) **Liquidity**: Are you able to get your money out, or is it locked in for an extended period of time? Some investments require a fixed holding period or they are extremely difficult to sell.
4) **Familiarity**: Do you know the person or firm offering you the investment? If you don't, or even if you do, it never hurts to check them out with your provincial securities commissions. The Investment Dealers Association is also a good place to start enquiries.
5) **Cost**: Everything has a price, whether it's out in the open for all to see, or if it's imbedded in the investment return. Make sure you understand how much a particular investment is going to cost you.
6) **Web only information**: While many companies are enjoying success on the internet, you really want to do your homework before signing up over the web. If the parent company is offshore and it's only presence in Canada is a web site, getting your money back could be a problem if anything goes wrong.
7) **Reluctance of any kind**: If someone is giving you a sales pitch, but starts to falter when you start to demand substantive information, a big red flag should shoot up. Legitimate investments in Canada are generally accompanied by reams of detailed information for you to peruse. A scam artist wants to provide as little real information as possible.

Gauging Your Progress

Now that you have a fairly clear handle on investing, you need to keep track of your progress. Some people choose to focus on a particular percentage return to judge the performance of their portfolio. While this is a very effective method of tracking portfolio performance, it doesn't necessarily give you the big picture.

You don't want to get bogged down in second guessing performance numbers over the short term when it may be that the market itself is largely responsible for a portfolio return that's less than you projected. What I'd like to propose is the use of a net worth statement to track your financial health and progress.

A net worth statement, just like any other aspect of financial planning, can be as simple or complex as you choose to make it. Basically, it is the sum of all of your assets minus your liabilities, so get an idea of what you own and take off what you owe - that's your net worth. Your net worth should grow fairly steadily from year to year, with exceptions occurring from time to time in the form of windfalls or unexpected, large expenses. The net worth statement simplifies what can be extremely complex investment return calculations by taking them out of the picture completely.

For instance, assume you have a loan for the purpose of investments and it's compounded on a monthly basis. Meanwhile the underlying investments themselves are experiencing capital gains, which may or may not be consistent. Calculating the real cost of the loan against the real return on the investment may take more time and effort than you're willing to spend. When you consider doing that for all of your investments and fixed assets, you can imagine that a lot of time will be used up struggling with the details that can be summarized fairly simply in a net worth statement. Simply put, if your net worth is growing at a rate faster than that of inflation, you're succeeding. If you project this growth out to your specific goals, you can see whether adjustments to your plan are warranted. Remember, when doing this always include a fudge factor either way for unexpected developments.

3
Insurance

"I detest life insurance agents; they always argue that I shall some day die, which is not so." Stephen Leacock

The goal of insurance isn't to increase your standard of living, but to *protect the standard of living you currently enjoy*. Funerals, disease, disabling accidents are subjects that make your stomach churn, so it's understandable that many people avoid talking to insurance providers. However, insurance is an integral part of a properly formulated financial plan, and insurance professionals in today's market understand that a client who feels that their agent is acting in his or her best interest will happily refer their friends and family. A professional insurance representative will seek only to recommend sufficient coverage tailored to suit your specific needs.

Risk Management

I won't go into the specifics of the different forms of insurance, as the subject could easily cover an entire book of its own. You've probably heard the expression risk management in association with insurance products and, in reality, that's all insurance is: The management of your personal exposure to risk. Insurance can seem confusing and mysterious because of the many variables used to calculate coverage and premiums. Variables such as your sex, age, smoking, drinking, sports, etc. all play a factor in determining how risky you are to insure and, just like investing, risk and return are directly related.

If you want to buy insurance from a company, you're essentially making a contract with that company that in the event of your death or disability, they will pay a certain amount of compensation to your dependants or whomever you've named as a beneficiary. The fee you pay must be reasonable to you for the security it brings, or you won't want to pay it. On the other hand, the insurance company looks at you and figures out using all of the above criteria and more, how likely it is that you'll either die or become disabled before the contract period is up, or before they've collected enough fees. So, if there's a high likelihood that you'll need the insurance money due to personal circumstances such as hereditary family diseases, job hazards, etc., premiums will be higher. If that probability is lower, premiums become lower.

You can take comfort knowing that neither you nor the insurance company wants you to be harmed in any way. A lot of people believe insurance is virtually like throwing money away, but I prefer to think of insurance as a helmet. If you never fall off your bike and bang your head, is the helmet a waste of money? No. Just like a helmet, insurance is there to make sure that if something were to happen, you won't be financially harmed.

Your goal as an insurance customer is to reduce the probability of financial loss through death or disability. So how much insurance is enough? A complete financial plan is an invaluable resource that will enable you to define your insurance needs. Completing your financial plan gives you an additional opportunity to review your plan and determine whether or not there would be a shortfall in your finances if you were to die or become disabled tomorrow. For many pre-retirement families death or injury could result in financial disaster.

What you need to look at is exactly how much income from savings or other sources would be coming in if you weren't able to work. Would this income cover you or your family's expenses, goals, and major purchases? If the answer is no, then you need to define the shortfall and calculate a payout amount that would allow you to cover these expenses.

Insurance in its basic form is the management of risk by sharing, transferring or retaining of the costs associated with the risk. However, insurance is just one method of risk control, there are others such as risk avoidance and risk reduction. In risk avoidance, the insurance company and you are primarily concerned with discretionary activities with high probability and high severity risks. For example, if you routinely skydive on the weekends, then your insurance provider has no choice but to increase your insurance premiums. A method of risk avoidance would be to choose a less risky hobby, such as basket weaving or lawn bowling. On the other hand, if you're not willing to give up your risky pursuits, risk reduction may be the answer. Take extra safety precautions; add an automatic chute deployment device. Or segregate the risk by taking out extra insurance specifically for one-time events thus preventing an unfortunate accident from causing a devastating financial loss to the family.

Life Insurance

No one buys life insurance for themselves. The benefits can't be taken with you; they go to your family, friends or business partners to take care of their needs after you have passed. In that way, purchasing life insurance is one of the most selfless acts you can make. When you buy life insurance, you're essentially doing one of two things: Creating an estate or replacing your ability to earn an income. When most people consider purchasing life insurance, they tend to dwell on the product itself, or worse, their ultimate demise. I prefer to think about who and what I'm buying it for. Life insurance allows someone without much in the way of substantial assets to pass along an estate to their heirs, or it could allow your family to continue in the kind of lifestyle they enjoyed while you were alive. It could send your children to college or wipe out your debts. Even the very wealthy buy life insurance because they realize that the cost of not having it may simply be too much.

When confronted with the prospect of life insurance, the first question most respond with is, "I know I need insurance, but how much do I really need"? The best answer to this question is to ask a financial planner or an insurance professional to provide an Insurance Needs Analysis. If you're still working, you'll generally want to purchase enough coverage to provide a lump sum sufficient to generate an income similar to the one you're earning until you retire. In addition, you'll want to cover your funeral expenses, any outstanding debts, and perhaps provide enough for an education or emergency fund depending on your circumstances. If you're retired, then it may simply be a matter of what kind of estate you decide to leave behind. Your insurance professional will likely go through a questionnaire to help determine adequate coverage while taking any existing coverage or savings into consideration. Once an amount is determined, the next step is to look at the various types of life insurance available. The three main types include term life, whole life and universal life.

Term life is generally the most cost effective way to provide coverage for a risk that will disappear or dwindle over time. If you're purchasing insurance to cover debts or your earning capacity, term life may be the best answer. However, if the risk you're insuring doesn't have an expiry date, then term life may not be the most cost-effective solution. Generally, term life is most efficient to protect against risks that last less than 20 years. Often term life policies have been likened to renting the insurance. Once you decide to stop paying the premiums, you have no residual value or ongoing coverage built up. Also, whenever you renew your policy, the premiums tend to increase, becoming more and more costly as you grow older.

Whole life insurance is more like owning than renting. As long as the policyholder pays the premiums, the insurance coverage will remain in place. If you were to compare the cost of a whole life policy during the initial stages, it would look very expensive when compared to equal coverage with a term life product. However, as the term life premiums rise over time, they gradually equal and then surpass the cost of the whole life premiums. In adding up the total cost of protecting yourself with term life for greater than 20 years;

whole life is actually more affordable. This is why whole life may be a better solution to protect against risks that may last longer than 20 years. In addition, a whole life policy builds up a cash value over time so, if you were to stop making premium payments, you may be eligible to receive some money back or to allow the cash surrender value to fund ongoing insurance coverage of some kind.

A third option would be universal life insurance. Universal-life is similar to whole life, but tends to be much more flexible in nature. The universal life policy can be changed periodically, subject to the approval of the insurance company. The investment aspect attached to the universal life policy may allow policy holders to choose among various investment vehicles themselves. A potential drawback to this flexibility is the chance that premiums may increase over time to provide the same amount of coverage due to fluctuations in investment performance, claims received by the insurance company, expenses, and more.

Mortgage Insurance

When you go to your bank for a mortgage, they'll often ask you if you would like to add mortgage life and disability insurance to your monthly payment. This form of insurance is relatively easy to obtain and often seems like a good idea because after all, you are protecting your estate against debt. However, there are a few things you need to be aware of with mortgage insurance. The largest issue is that the insurance benefit decreases in tandem with the value of the mortgage as it is paid down. This may not seem like a big deal during the first few years where you're paying mostly interest on the mortgage, but as you go along you end up continuing to pay for coverage you're no longer receiving. For example, let's say you take out a mortgage for $200,000 and you purchase mortgage insurance. After a few years you manage to pay it down to $180,000 but continue to pay the same insurance premiums. If you were to pass away at this point, $180,000 is all the insurance money you would receive. Actually, the bank would get the death benefit directly and use it to pay off the mortgage. However, if you had purchased $200,000 of private life insurance, your designated beneficiary would have received $200,000 to pay off the mortgage and use the remainder for whatever purposes necessary.

A second issue with mortgage insurance is that while it appears to be fairly inexpensive at first, it tends to be more expensive overall. And since the lender holds the contract with the insurance company, the rates can be changed or the plan cancelled at any time. Also, perhaps you were to change lenders in a move or to get a better mortgage rate. The mortgage insurance you had previously would terminate with the old mortgage and you may have to re-qualify, often at higher rates.

If you're taking out a mortgage or considering insurance coverage of any kind, it's generally a good idea to speak with an insurance specialist to get a comparison before you buy.

Disability Insurance

While many of us plan some form of insurance for loss of life, disability insurance is often overlooked even though in many ways it represents the greatest danger to your financial health. Lets say you were killed in an accident and didn't have insurance. Your significant other may not be able to enjoy the lifestyle he or she is accustomed to and may experience additional expenses but, even without insurance, at some point there is the possibility that he or she can get on with their life. Now imagine you became severely disabled instead.

Depending on the degree of disability, you and your spouse may become trapped in the spiral of a declining lifestyle. If your disability was fairly minor or short lived, perhaps the setback would be moderate. However, if the disability was chronic or such that you were unable to care for yourself, without adequate coverage, the effect could be catastrophic. For instance, if you were the primary breadwinner and had a spouse and children, the expenses would only increase. Your normal expenses would continue, but the additional expense of hospital bills or in-home care could combine to cripple your finances. Couple that with the possibility that you and your spouse don't have a Power of Attorney over each other's finances, and other ugly situations begin to pop up. The money may be there but, if your spouse can't access it, he or she will have to work through a public trustee and justify every move they make.

The purpose of disability insurance is to provide the insured with investment capital and related income to replace the loss of earned income. But many people feel that the cost of this insurance is prohibitive compared to life insurance. The reason for the greater cost is, of course, that you're much more likely to become disabled over your lifetime than to be killed. That fact alone should suggest that disability insurance is a necessity rather than just "a nice to have". As with life insurance, disability insurance premiums are determined by a number of factors relative to the individual and the type of insurance being purchased. While insurance companies restrict the amount of benefit received to between 50% and 70% of earned income before tax, rest assured that your net income should remain close to the same level, as the insurance proceeds are non-taxable.

Government Assistance

Private insurance isn't necessarily your only protection. A disability pension is provided to Canada Pension Plan (CPP) participants who are unable to work due to a severe and prolonged physical or mental condition. These payments continue until age 65 at which time they are converted to retirement pensions, or until recovery from the disability. Also, all workers covered by the government Employment Insurance (EI) plan are entitled to a sickness benefit in case of illness, injury or quarantine. People who are employed and pay into EI are covered, however self-employed personnel are not. Owners are encouraged to ensure that they are adequately covered through private sources. CPP disability coverage as well as EI benefits are treated as taxable income. The Worker's Compensation Board (WCB) also provides some disability coverage, but these benefits cover only those injuries or sicknesses that are job related. Unlike CPP and EI, WCB benefits are not classed as taxable income.

Long-term Care

With the increase in life expectancy and improved medical care, people are living longer than ever before. If you have an elderly dependant who requires care, the resulting financial obligations can wipe out your life savings. Should you seek the appropriate professional care, it may not even be affordable. The average stay in a long-term care facility is almost three months, with a cost of between $3,000 and $6,000 per month. Government subsidies may ease the burden, but not completely. Even if there is a government nursing home in your area, during times of government cutbacks the wait list may be as long as nine months. Long-term care insurance was created recently to address the enormous cost associated with the health care of the aged. But as with any form of insurance, individuals should purchase coverage *before* age, disease, or incapacity limits their ability to pass underwriting standards. You aren't completely on your own, since every provincial and territorial government in Canada has a hospital plan based on the minimum requirements of the federal Canada Health Act. The services covered under insured services are defined as services that are medically required and rendered by qualified health professionals.

Critical Illness Insurance

While provincial health plans cover most basic hospital and medical costs, extended health plans offered by private companies pick up the slack for coverage required in excess of the provincial plans or expenses not covered. Often, employers offer the plans as a benefit of employment. If you're self-employed, however, you'll need to purchase private health insurance through a private insurance company.

Related to long-term care insurance, critical illness insurance is one of the newer forms of health care coverage being offered by insurance companies. Recent statistics have determined that, before the age of 65, Canadians are ten times more likely to be unable to work due to critical illness than die. One of the big attractions of critical illness insurance is that the beneficiary receives a lump sum upon diagnosis, and may use it however he or she sees fit.

Insurance can easily be viewed as an unwanted or unnecessary extra expense, but part of financial planning is to prepare for events that can't be controlled. Ask someone who has experienced a devastating loss or disability if they had insurance. They're glad they did. If they didn't, they rue the day they said, "Nah, I'll take my chances."

4
Education Planning

"The only thing new is the history you don't know."

Harry S. Truman

Many of my clients want to provide their children with opportunities that they didn't have when they were younger. Education planning, as with any form of planning, enables them to save and grow money to cover the ever-increasing costs of attending a major post secondary institution. Before you begin saving though, do a little research. How likely is it that your child will want to pursue further education once high school is over, and what type of education would that be? Also, if you're not happy with the classroom sizes and caliber of instruction in the public school system, private schooling can be an effective but very expensive alternative.

University has a reputation for being expensive and, next to public school, it is. However, be aware that university education is heavily subsidized in Canada, so if your child wants to attend Berkley or Harvard in the U.S., hope for a scholarship, as the fees are substantially higher. Community colleges have become more and more popular of late, as skills learned there are generally thought of as more job specific and increase hiring potential. Many of these programs are shorter than a full university degree, but can be extremely expensive compared to university tuition. Aside from the actual cost of tuition, you must be prepared for books that cost almost as much as the courses themselves. Add meal and housing costs for students who wish to move away from home to study, and you can see how the expenses begin to add up.

Just like saving for retirement, putting money aside for education is a practice best begun early. The longer your money has to work for you, the less you actually have to contribute and the less stress it will place on your finances. Ideally, you'll want to have the funding of your child's post secondary education completed by the time he or she hits high school. If you're a little late in getting started, and you're actually close to needing the money to subsidize your child's education, then perhaps another approach is necessary. Have your advisor help you prepare a cash flow statement. This will allow you to recognize areas of expense that may be trimmed or eliminated altogether. Also, ask your advisor to look into financial aid options such as grants, scholarships, loans, or work-study programs. And perhaps your child may be expected to help with some of the tuition costs.

Registered Education Savings Plan

One popular form of saving for educational costs is the Registered Education Savings Plan (RESP). These were first introduced by the government in 1964 as an incentive to increase savings for post secondary education. The main appeal of RESPs is that no tax deduction arises from a contribution, and the investments accumulate within the plan on a tax-free basis. Once paid out, income generated is taxed in the hands of the student, who generally has a much lower marginal tax rate than the subscriber. The beneficiary must use these funds to pay for their post secondary education expenses.

There are two basic forms of these plans commonly available. The non-family plan can only have one beneficiary who is unrestricted, meaning that anyone can be a beneficiary of this type of plan. However, the family plan differs in that it can have one or more beneficiaries who must be connected by blood or adoption to each living subscriber or have been connected to a deceased original subscriber. In both plans, the subscriber is free to decide when and how much he wants to contribute, and may decide to take a break in contributions at any time.

To increase the attractiveness of RESPs, Canadian Educational Savings Grants (CESG) give an RESP beneficiary under the age of 18 a 20% grant on the money contributed for the year to a maximum of $2,000 per year. In the event that the beneficiary does not attend post secondary school, it is possible for the subscriber to rollover the accumulated investment income to his or her RRSP or simply withdraw it subject to income tax and a penalty tax.

RESPs have some disadvantages; they're a little inflexible. RESP investments must be used to fund post secondary education and subscribers face a forfeiture of income under some plans if the beneficiary doesn't continue their education. There are a number of alternatives to RESPs if these restrictions seem too tight but, regardless of what product you're using to save money, a regular contribution plan is an excellent way to begin.

Some people choose to bank the child tax credit when it is received, specifically for the purpose of providing for their child's education. By setting up a bank account in the child's name and depositing the child tax credit payments to that account, parents can thus ensure that the income is taxed in the hands of the child. This can in turn create a larger after tax pool of funds to finance the child's education.

Trusts

Family trusts are less popular now due to income attribution rules that eliminate the advantages of income splitting. However, because this attribution doesn't apply to capital gains generated by children under the age of 18, they can still be a useful tool in providing for your child's education. It should be noted that a family trust comes with significant administration and set-up fees, so the cost to create this vehicle may outweigh its potential benefit. There is a less formal and inexpensive alternative, however.

If you opened a mutual fund account under an informal trust in the child's name, the first year of interest and dividend income would be attributed back to the parent, but the child would be taxed on any subsequent capital gains. It should be mentioned that capital gain generating instruments generally have greater volatility and can result in a significant reduction in assets available for the education costs should the market take a downturn just prior to the time of financial need.

Other Sources of Funding

Under certain circumstances, it may be impossible for parents to gather sufficient funds for their children's education, so other sources of cash must be examined. Traditionally students have turned to the Canada Student Loan Program and to other similar programs offered in their respective provinces. However, a number of financial institutions have created programs that are specifically targeted for students and provide greater flexibility than conventional borrowing. Additionally, many academic institutions offer scholarships, bursaries and loans based on need or academic performance. The sad truth about scholarships is that many of these opportunities are left unclaimed merely because no one bothered to apply or assumed you had to have straight A's to qualify, so take the time to research your options. Also, the children of parents working in many large Canadian companies have special scholarships set up to help them. Often corporations are looking to contribute to education, but prefer for it to be offered inhouse, so a call to your Human Resources Department may be well worth your time.

Lifelong Learning Plan

Recently, the government created a new program to aid in acquiring education in the form of the Lifelong Learning Plan (LLP). The LLP allows you withdraw up to $10,000 a year from your RRSPs to provide monetary assistance for the education of you or your spouse or commonlaw partner. Unfortunately, you cannot use the LLP for your child's education. The total withdrawal from your RRSP plan cannot exceed $20,000. The money drawn from your RRSPs is not included in income and, as such, is not taxed; much like the First Time Homebuyer's Program. The total withdrawal must be repaid over a period not exceeding ten years, and any amount still not repaid at the end of that period becomes included in your income. Usually the payment amount is one-tenth of the total amount you withdrew until the full amount is paid. There are conditions however, as the student must enroll full time in a qualified educational program at a designated educational institution. If the student has a disability, he or she may be enrolled on a part-time basis.

5
Retirement Planning

"I came solely with the design to simplify my way of life and to secure the independence through which I could be enabled to remain true to myself." Thomas Carlyle in a letter to Goethe, 1828

Probably 90% of my clients see planning for their retirement as the focus of their financial plan. While the other 10% may already be retired, they too need to plan how they approach their post-retirement finances. As the cost of living keeps going up, it makes it very difficult for many Canadians to find the spare money to invest in their future. It also makes living on a fixed income even more challenging after retirement. If you're interested in retiring before the magical age of 65, when Canada Pension Plan (CPP) and Old Age Security (OAS) benefits begin to kick in, it becomes even more difficult.

Fifty years ago, a family expected to pay off their mortgage somewhere in their mid fourties and do it on a single income. Currently, the majority of Canadian households rely on two breadwinners (either full or part-time), and still don't expect to pay off their mortgage until their late fifties. Why? Part of it is the fact that the cost of living has gone up. The other is that our expectations for our standard of living have increased as well. Fifty years ago we all managed to survive with one TV, one car, and a 1,200 square foot home. Nowadays, many of us aren't satisfied without a big house, two cars and three TVs. Now all this doesn't mean you should give up on your dreams of early retirement, just that careful planning is necessary.

Shifting Into Retirement Mode

If you do hope to retire early, you must first contemplate the challenges that this brings. Obviously, the primary concern is that you'll have a longer retirement period to fund, but you might also want to consider what else you'd like to do with your time afterwards. Lets assume you have an expected lifetime of 25 years after you retire. For some of us, sitting on the beach, drinking margaritas would get boring pretty quickly. If you're a self-proclaimed workaholic, down shifting from fifth gear to park may be a little too abrupt for your system to handle. Easing into retirement may satisfy two goals: Increasing leisure time and generating a modest income. A lower stress, lower income job may allow you to get the additional relaxation time you deserve, while still proving a form of supplementary income to help stretch out your savings. Even part-time or volunteer work can ease the transition, while allowing the time for the development of sports or hobbies that had been on the back-burner for your primary working years. After you feel that this period of your semi-retirement has played out, perhaps then you may be ready to make the final move into full retirement.

In structuring your finances to allow early retirement, consider not only your potential remaining lifetime, but also at the quality of life you can honestly expect to experience. Various health issues may conspire to increase your personal cost of living due to expenses for nursing care or hospitalization. No one likes to contemplate a severe decline in health, but my philosophy is that preparing for the worst lets you enjoy the best of life without financial worry.

Budgeting

There is a prevailing notion that you need to have one million dollars in your RRSPs by the time you stop working to finance a comfortable retirement. This may be too much or it may be too little; it all depends on what you want to do when you retire and what other sources of income you have. First of all, you should determine what kind of income you will need when you're retired.

A rule of thumb suggests you'll need 70% of your current income during retirement, but that changes based on a number of factors. If you want to live exactly the same lifestyle as you have right now, 70% may work. Remember this figure assumes that you have paid off your house and other large debts. Now if you want to travel extensively or take up an expensive hobby such as golf, you may wish to increase that budget somewhat. If you intend to lead a fairly sedentary retirement and your major expense to this point was saving for retirement, you may wish to lower that target.

To get an accurate idea of what you'll need, sit back and seriously consider what you want to be doing when you retire. If your interests require more or less money, then adjust your projected expenses accordingly. You should have a fairly good idea of what you'll absolutely need, but it's always a good idea to build in a margin of error for any unforeseen or forgotten expenses. Again, a trusted financial advisor can make this task quite simple for you. Considering your desired lifestyle and allowing for some unexpected expenses, you can formulate a rough idea of how much you'll need to retire on.

Women's Studies

It should come as no surprise to most that women are different than men. As such, any retirement strategies for women should take these differences into consideration. On average, women live seven years longer than men. As these extra years tend to come toward the end of their lives, women need more money to fund a longer retirement. The average age of retirement for women in Canada is 58. This is approximately three years earlier than the average retirement age for men. Sadly, the average age of widowhood for women is also 58 and *senior women have the highest rate of low income of any age group in Canada*.

Compounding the previously mentioned challenges, women tend to be out of the labor force more due to family and child rearing. This impacts them in the form of lost wages, which leads to lower

RRSP and pension contribution room as well as lower participation in government plans like the Canada Pension Plan.

What all of this means to women is that, as a group, women *need* to be putting away approximately 12% of their gross income every year as opposed to the widely held standard of 10%. While generalities are useful if you plan to have a rough idea of how much to save, I would highly recommend that *the best plan is to have a plan*. Work with a financial planner to determine exactly how to achieve the kind of retirement you want.

Testing Uncertainty in Your Plan

Now that you have a rough idea of your retirement income needs, test it.

If the economy deteriorates, will that destroy your savings? Average returns give you a fairly accurate guide of what to expect from your investments, but they fail to show how a market drop can impact your principal in the short term. Certainly, a market recovery can reduce or erase those losses over time, but if time is short or you're drawing on principal during the downturn, there may not be enough assets left to build on.

How will inflation affect your purchasing power? Often when we project our retirement savings balances out to 30 years, we smile while thinking of its huge proportions due to the miracle of compounded returns. However, often we fail to see that the cost of living compounds as well, and that huge savings fund may not be as comparatively large as we may have thought. Please be sure to take inflation into consideration when determining the income you'll need to survive on once retired.

Will the Canada Pension Plan and the Old Age Security system still be there when you retire? The debate rages on whether or not the Government of Canada can or will continue to fund these programs. The CPP is your money. You contribute to it on every paycheque so the government has to give you something, even if it's a lump sum payout should they decide to close it down. The OAS is a bit trickier. Essentially, the OAS is a form of social support, which is in place to ensure a certain minimum standard of living. However, as you don't pay directly into the plan (taxes form an indirect contribution), such support can be removed without any great fanfare. I strongly advise clients not to count on the OAS to supplement their income due to the uncertainly that surrounds it. If you retire and reap its benefits, great. If not, at least you'll be prepared.

Registered Plans

Now that you've determined how much you'll need, taking unforeseen occurrences into account, what products are available to get you there? By far, the most well known and utilized would be the Registered Retirement Savings Plan (RRSP). While most people are quite familiar with this plan, I'd like to take a closer look. An RRSP, allows you to shelter income from tax. Since the investment returns (interest, dividends and capital gains) are not reduced by tax when held within an RRSP, your **registered investments** are able to grow at a far faster rate than if they were **non-registered**. So it makes sense for Canadians to contribute as much as possible to their RRSP accounts as laid out according to the Income Tax Act. The key to RRSPs is to realize that while they do grow much more quickly than non-registered investments, *the entire withdrawal amount is subject to your current marginal tax rate when withdrawn, while withdrawals from non-registered investments are taxed only on the income they generate*. So avoid having an inflated impression of your net worth by not subtracting the tax due from the investment should you choose to draw money from the fund.

Registered Investment – Investments held within an account, recognized by the Canada Customs and Revenue Agency, that defers paying income tax on the earnings of the account until the funds are redeemed or drawn from the plan.

Non-Registered Investments – Investments held in accounts that are not included in a registered plan as recognized by the Canada Customs and Revenue Agency.

Value of RRSPs

Aside from the benefits of tax sheltered growth and immediate tax deductions on contribution, there is an additional advantage to registered savings. Generally, when you're contributing to your RRSPs, your marginal tax rate is higher than it will likely be in your retirement years. As such, deferring the tax on income contributed to the plan results in you having to *pay less tax when you draw the income out at retirement*. Now, deferred tax growth may be all well and good if you're in your 30's or 40's, but what if you're among the many Canadians in their 50's and 60's?

Is there any value in contributing to your RRSPs at an age where tax-free growth has a steadily shrinking time horizon? Yes, but for different reasons. If you're a younger individual, the value of tax-deferred growth is pretty obvious, but your income tends to be lower *on average* than your older counterparts. So while it may be mentioned that a tax deduction is another big benefit of investing in RRSPs, it won't be the focus of the conversation. However, as you draw nearer to the golden years, these priorities tend to flip-flop. No longer are you as concerned with tax-deferred growth as you are with the available tax deduction to offset your increasing earnings capacity. So if you're maximizing your RRSP contribution at $16,500 for the 2005 tax year and inhabit a tax bracket close to the 50% mark, you're immediate return would be somewhere in the area of $8,250; an amount the underlying investments will take much longer to generate. At a lower tax bracket, such as when you were beginning your career, you wouldn't be earning enough to reach the $16,500 mark in available contributions and your marginal tax rate being lower, would result in the immediate return being less significant than the tax-deferred growth. It should be noted here that the RRSP contribution limit has been raised twice in recent federal budgets, and should reach $18,000 by the 2006 tax year. Always check on updated information before implementing your plans.

Diversification

Previously, I mentioned the importance of diversification in your investments. This is not a new concept, nor will it come as any great surprise that I advocate a well-diversified portfolio. But the truth is, whether Canadians believe it or not, most *do not* have a well-diversified portfolio. The asset allocation theory suggests that it's not necessarily the specific underlying investments, but the *proportion* of the three basic asset classes (cash, fixed income, and equities) that's responsible for the bulk of your return over time. Spreading your investments over these classes represents the most basic level of diversification.

You can have money in 100 different companies, but if they're all equities, you're not adequately diversified by asset class. Even the most aggressive asset allocation portfolio has at least 10% invested in an asset other than equities. The thinking behind this form of diversification is that not one of the three asset classes has been the top performer year to year. Equities certainly provide the best return in the long run, but as we saw at the turn of the millennium, fixed income is capable of being the top performer in a given year as well. In the late 1980s, cash was actually the top performing asset class. Once your asset mix is set up, you can look towards diversifying by other factors.

Sector diversification is another important method. For example, while putting all of your money in the tech sector seemed like a good idea in 1999, it soon proved to be an empty promise that hurt a lot of investors.

Style diversification has made a resurgence of late. Some fund managers approach their fund management with an eye to purchasing rapidly growing companies with a quick in and out approach, while other managers prefer to buy and hold companies that represent long-term value. As well, investors now have the opportunity to diversify into passively managed funds that mirror stock indices and offer a lower priced alternative to actively managed funds.

Maximizing Your Foreign Content

Canadians, as with pretty much every other nationality in the world, have a national bias. This means they invest the majority of their money in Canadian companies and investments. It may be that emotions, in the form of pride and loyalty, keep many Canadians investing in Canadian companies and products. It may also be that people tend to invest in what they know, and many of us are far more aware of the current status of the companies and investments in the country in which we live. Regardless of the reasons, Canada, while the second largest country in the world by landmass, makes up only around 2% of the world market. So, investing in countries other than Canada can benefit you with geographic diversification. Why? Because while Canada may be experiencing a recession, Europe might be prospering. Also, from a strictly historical point of view, the stock market in Canada has returned approximately 10% on average, whereas the U.S. has returned closer to 13%.

Even though I don't recommend keeping all of your money invested in Canada, I wouldn't advocate moving it all to U.S. funds either as foreign exchange and specific market risks are issues to consider. In 2005 the Federal Government finally eliminated foreign content restrictions altogether for registered accounts and pensions. Previously, the maximum allowable was 30%, which meant that if you had more than 30% in foreign investments within your registered plan you would have to pay a penalty. The premise behind this was to keep Canadians investing in Canadian companies. However, as most Canadians haven't maximized their foreign content anyway, the change will likely have little impact. However, it should simplify investing decisions since the **derivative** or "clone" funds will no longer be necessary to achieve greater foreign content and, over time, will be eliminated from mutual fund companys' portfolios.

Derivative Securities – A security whose value is determined by the value of some other security or asset. An example of a derivative security would be an option or future.

So just how much should you place in non-Canadian investments? For adequate diversification, a good policy is to have anywhere from 30% to 45% invested outside of Canada. Once again, work with a professional investment advisor to help determine the right level of foreign content for your portfolio. While diversifying your portfolio with foreign investments can lower regional market risks, it does add other risks in the form of foreign currency exchange fluctuations. A recent example is the run-up of the Canadian dollar in 2004, which impacted the overall performance of foreign investments.

Tax Strategies

Canadians feel the effect of taxes on almost everything, but they have an especially large effect on the long-term growth of an investment portfolio. You don't have a great deal of control over the tax effectiveness of investments in your Registered Retirement Savings Plan (RRSP) or Registered Retirement Income Fund (RRIF). Regardless of how income is generated within the RRSP umbrella, once you remove funds, tax is applied at your *full marginal tax rate.* On the other hand, if you have both registered and non-registered investments earmarked for the same goal (e.g. retirement), then you can implement some strategies for tax effectiveness. As you now know, any investments that generate interest income are taxed at your full marginal tax rate. However, investments in Canadian corporations that generate *dividends* are *favored* by the Income Tax Act with the **dividend tax credit** and, as such, experience a tax rate that is much better than that of interest bearing securities. While the capital gains tax reduction didn't get much press at the time, equities get the best tax treatment of all, where any capital gains generated are only 50% taxable at your current marginal tax rate. Pulling this together, you can structure your entire portfolio, both registered and non-registered investments to take advantage of the tax behavior of your various investments.

Once you've determined how you're going to allocate out your total portfolio, try to house as much of the interest bearing investments within your RRSP or RRIF as they're fully taxable regardless. Now you can use the tax advantages of your dividends and capital gains bearing investments in your non-registered portfolio. Rest assured, I'm not suggesting you should reduce your RRSP holdings; just that if you do have non-registered investments as part of your overall portfolio, ensure that they're more tax efficient.

Dividend Tax Credit – Refers to the preferential tax treatment granted to dividend income (common and preferred) received from taxable Canadian corporations. The dividend is grossed up by 25% and the tax credit of 13.33% is based on this amount.

Retirement tax planning also offers the opportunity to split income with your spouse. The spousal RRSP plan allows you to contribute to an RRSP plan set up in your spouse's name. Any spousal contributions are still deducted from your RRSP contribution room, so no increased contribution allowance is gained through the practice. What is gained, if done properly, is that funds drawn from RRSPs and RRIFs are taxed at a lower tax rate. Very important to this practice, is the tax bracket of the contributing individual as compared to his or her spouse. Basically, it boils down to this: If you expect to have income in a *higher* tax bracket at retirement than your spouse, then you should be making the spousal RRSP contributions.

The general idea is to split eventual income between spouses to take advantage of lower tax rates. For example, assume you were the primary breadwinner, and you had a nice pension that still left RRSP contribution room after the pension adjustment. Lets also speculate that your spouse has an income at a lower tax bracket. Projecting the combination of all sources of income at retirement, you can see that you will still be in the higher tax bracket. Making spousal RRSP contributions allows your spouse to claim the income on his or her tax return when the funds are drawn at retirement. So you get

Attribution Rules – The attribution rules with respect to spouses provide that where property (including money) is transferred or loaned, directly or indirectly by you to your spouse, then all income or loss from the property, and any capital gain or loss on the disposition of the property will be attributed back to you.

the tax break in the higher tax bracket on contribution, and the funds are taxed less upon withdrawal than they would have otherwise been. It's a win-win situation. There are, however, a couple of things to remember. First of all, if you make a contribution to a spousal plan and these funds are withdrawn from the plan within two years of this contribution the income is **attributed back** to you. So if you think you're two years from retirement, assess your options carefully. Also, once contributed to your spouse's plan, the funds no longer legally belong to you. Be aware of the possible loss of these funds in the event of marital strife.

Drawing on Your Savings

By the end of the year in which you turn 69, you must either cash out your RRSPs or convert them into a RRIF. Cashing out is generally not a viable option. One of the major attractions of RRSPs is that the income you would have otherwise paid tax on when it was contributed to the plan may be drawn out when you're enjoying a lower tax bracket. By taking all of your money out of your RRSPs at the same time, you'd immediately have to pay income tax at the highest marginal tax rate (depending on the size of your RRSP portfolio). A more viable solution is RRIFing.

A RRIF, or Registered Retirement Income Fund, shelters your investments from taxation until the funds are withdrawn, much like an RRSP. The differences are that a RRIF requires you to withdraw a minimum amount each year and no contributions can be made to the account, except in the conversion of additional RRSP accounts. Certainly, you can withdraw more from a RRIF if you need additional income; but the minimum has to be drawn.

A RRIF account allows a wide variety of investments to be held just like an RRSP, however a RRIF also allows the purchase of **life or fixed term annuities**. If you want to retire earlier than 69 and use your RRSP savings as a source of income, you can convert your RRSPs into RRIFs at any time. You can also have an RRSP and RRIF account existing concurrently, so you can continue to make contributions. Once you've determined how much you intend to withdraw from your RRIF as a source of income, you need to determine when you want to receive the funds.

RRIF account withdrawals may be made on either a monthly or annual basis. Monthly withdrawals may be of greater benefit, for two reasons. First of all, it provides you with a cash flow that closely resembles that which you enjoyed while employed. But more importantly, if you have a diversified portfolio of investments and funds are drawn only once a year, you fall to the mercy of the market as to the valuation of the investments at that specific point in time. Monthly withdrawals act like a reverse dollar cost averaging, and lessen the chance of drawing on the funds at a low point in the market.

Life or Fixed Term Annuities – An annuity that is paid out over a predetermined number of years up to age 90, or for a maximum of 20 years.

While you've managed to build up your RRSPs and converted to a RRIF, you may want to consider minimizing the withdrawals from this plan should you have *additional* non-registered investments to draw an income from. Ideally, you'll want to structure the majority of your investment withdrawals as follows.

Start with the non-registered investments owned by the highest tax bracket spouse. You'd want to reduce these first, because you're paying the most tax on them of all your investments. Second, draw on the non-registered investments of the lower income spouse. You want to eliminate the non-registered investments first, as they generate taxable income even if no withdrawals are being taken. Once those have been eliminated, start in on the registered funds of the lower income spouse. This delays paying the most tax on the funds held by the higher income spouse. Finally, once these funds are exhausted, begin drawing on the registered funds held by the higher income spouse. Delaying this as long as possible will help keep your total tax payable down. You may not have a lot of choice when it comes to your RRIFs, as you're required to draw the minimum after you've turned 69, however, any additional income needs should be addressed by the strategies for drawing on your savings as outlined above.

Annuities

Should you be uncomfortable with the fluctuations in the value of mutual funds, or the reinvestment risk associated with GICs, then annuities may provide an alternative investment vehicle for your retirement income. In choosing to purchase an annuity, you're essentially buying an income stream. Annuities can appear to offer a greater return on investment compared to GICs of similar rate due to their higher periodic payments. While this seems instantly attractive, remember that an annuity payment includes both interest and principal, while most GIC payments are made up solely of interest.

In choosing an annuity for an income stream, you have to remember that aside from the principal invested, the payment amount is determined by the timing and duration of payments, as well as whether the annuity will continue to pay out after the annuitant has passed away. When purchasing an unregistered annuity with cash or funds from a non-registered account, only the interest generated by the annuity is taxable.

Registered annuities, on the other hand, are annuities that have been purchased with funds from a registered plan such as a pension, RRSP or RRIF account. Because no tax has yet been paid on the money in these plans, the principal and interest portions of the receipts from a registered annuity *are treated as taxable income*.

Annuities are most readily associated with insurance companies, and this is due to their sole ability to sell life annuities. Only life insurance companies can offer life annuities as the duration of the principal and interest payments is linked directly to the estimated lifespan of the annuitant, regardless of how long or short that may be. This form of annuity derives the payment schedule largely from actuarial tables, where the provider is essentially betting that you will pass away before the payments cut into their profits. So, the longer you live with this type of plan, the more bang you're getting for your buck.

Life annuities can come with guaranteed terms and guaranteed premium return options but, as you might expect, these have the effect of reducing the amount of payments. While only insurance companies can offer life annuities, other financial institutions as well as life insurance companies are able to provide term certain annuities. With either plan you're exchanging your cash for a contract that the principal will be repaid with interest over a set period of time. The annuitant is generally the purchaser, but may be another individual, such as a spouse or child, depending on your circumstances. A term certain annuity guarantees that payments will continue regardless of the death of the annuitant. If death occurs prior to the completion of the term, then a designated beneficiary receives the payments.

An annuity can also be indexed or non-indexed. Of course, it would be preferable to have an annuity indexed, as it provides for increases in the cost of living by increasing the payments over time. This increase may be a fixed percentage year-by-year, or linked directly to the Consumer Price Index (CPI). There is a drawback to indexing, as the payments are smaller in the first few years to make up for the contractual obligation to increase over time. In comparison, a non-indexed annuity has none of these features and does not increase payments over time.

Finally, annuities can be either immediate or deferred. Once you've purchased an immediate annuity, you usually begin to receive income payments from the plan one month after the annuity is purchased. However, a deferred annuity may be set up so that payments do not commence until a predetermined time, usually greater than one year from the time of purchase. The benefit of a deferred annuity is that the principal amount purchased creates interest income during the deferral period. However, because deferred annuities are still investments, the accrued interest must be declared on the anniversary date of the annuity purchase, with exception to annuities purchased prior to 1990, which may declare on a tri-annual basis. Further, deferred annuities may be subdivided into accumulation, pure, and survivorship annuities.

An accumulation annuity involves a single premium, a series of premiums, or varying amounts of premiums accumulated to provide a lump sum at a specific date set by the annuitant. The policyholder has the option of rolling the funds into a variety of dates or taking the cash surrender value. It's kind of like a save up plan. You make regular contributions to this plan with the idea of either taking it all out at the end or using the accumulated funds to purchase a regular annuity.

This contrasts with the inflexible pure deferred annuity, which may only provide fixed annuity payments at the end of the deferral period. This variety of annuity doesn't give you the option of taking the cash at the end; you have to roll over into a regular annuity.

Finally, a survivorship annuity is payable during the lifetime of one individual, but payment is deferred until after the death of another designated individual. This final form of annuity is rarely used now, due to its highly inflexible nature. Suppose you purchased the annuity to provide for your spouse in the event of your death, but your spouse passes away first. The policy would terminate without value and the annuity cannot be commuted, as there is no cash surrender value.

Insured Annuities

A slightly more complex strategy for maximizing your retirement income, but one that shouldn't be overlooked, is that of the insured annuity. This is not a single product, but rather the combination of two that creates a locked-in, fixed return investment that has become quite attractive to senior investors. The idea is to provide a superior return on investment over the more traditional fixed income products, while preserving the capital for the named beneficiaries.

So how does it work? Essentially, an investor would purchase an annuity that provides a regular payment stream to the investor as long as he or she are alive. Because this payment stream is calculated based on the underwriters' mortality tables plus a return of capital incorporated into the regular payment, the income produced is usually significantly higher and more tax effective than a similar amount invested in a GIC. The investor would also purchase a permanent life insurance policy with a death benefit equal to the amount invested in the annuity. The basis of this strategy is that the cost of the insurance is covered by a portion of the income from the annuity. At death, the annuity payments cease and the life insurance benefit is paid to the investor's estate or the named beneficiary. The net result generally being a significantly higher income stream when compared to other fixed rate products, with the added benefit of providing an estate for your beneficiaries.

As this is quite a complex investment strategy, I'll give an example of how it works compared to a 5% GIC. Assume the investor is a 70 year old, female, non-smoker with $500,000 to invest. We'll use 45% as her tax rate to keep it simple, and a $500,000 **Term-to-100** life insurance policy. Please keep in mind that the annuity payment and insurance cost would vary from individual to individual.

	Insured Annuity	**GIC**
Total Funds Available	$500,000	$500,000
Annual Payment	$43,095	$25,000
Taxable Amount	$12,039	$25,000
Tax Payable	$5,418	$11,250
Cash Flow Before Insurance Premium	$37,677	$13,750
Annual Term-to-100 Premium	$17,412	$0
Annual Net Cash Flow	**$20,265**	**$13,750**
Estate Value	$500,000	$500,000

As you can see, the insured annuity preserves the principal for the beneficiaries like the GIC, but also increases the annual net cash flow by 47%.

While an insured annuity provides a guaranteed income for life with preferential tax treatment compared with other guaranteed investments, it does come with some risk. Once the strategy is implemented, the funds are locked up for the life of the annuitant. Should investment market conditions or the owner's financial situation change dramatically, the life insurance contract may be cancelled but the annuity contract generally cannot be broken. Because of this lifetime commitment, this strategy tends to be more appropriate for investors of 60 years or older. Also, because of the preferential tax treatment, the insured annuity is particularly appropriate for investors with non-registered funds available for investment purposes that would have otherwise been taxed at high marginal tax rates.

While some insurance companies will issue a life insurance policy based on the existence of an annuity, it is generally advisable for the investor to be in sufficiently good health to qualify for life insurance on their own. As annuity contracts cannot generally be cashed in or broken, it is advisable to acquire the life insurance policy before committing to the annuity portion of the strategy.

Both the annuity and life insurance contracts should be underwritten as separate contracts. If they are treated as one product, the Canada Revenue Agency could conceivably suggest that the life insurance death benefit be non-exempt and subject to taxation where the cash value exceeds the adjusted cost base.

An insured annuity can be an attractive strategy for more mature investors looking for long-term, guaranteed returns. However, it is highly recommended that a prospective investor understand the risks and benefits of this strategy and obtain a personalized quote from the underwriter before committing to any action. As with any investment strategy, it is recommended that insured annuities be discussed with a qualified investment advisor or financial planner.

Other Sources of Income

Often when an individual is considering their retirement cash flow they ignore one of their largest sources of equity, *their home*. Reverse mortgages, offered by many financial institutions, allow you to use the equity in your home as a source of regular income while delaying the repayment of the debt until sometime in the future. There are two types of reverse mortgages, *fixed and lifetime*.

In a fixed mortgage, you borrow the funds against your home, and then repay the financial institution with principal and interest accrued to the settlement date. A lifetime plan is settled in a similar fashion by your estate once you have passed away. Of course in both circumstances you must repay the mortgage if you decide to sell your house prior to the completion of the mortgage. Financial institutions allow you to register against your home from 10% to 45% of its value, depending on your age. The older you are, the greater amount you can access. Regardless of the amount of equity you choose to utilize, you're still able to reside in your home for the duration of the plan or remainder of your life, depending on the type of reverse mortgage you've chosen. Once the money has been disbursed to your account, you're essentially free to do with it whatever you choose, investing it to generate an income, or gifting it to your children so that they can buy a home.

I have to stress that this income option is not one to be entered into lightly. Depending on the amount you borrow and the length of time you hold it, a reverse mortgage can seriously erode the equity in your home due to the compounding interest on the balance. For example, if you had a **clear title** house worth $100,000 and were able to get 45% of its value in a Home Equity Loan, based on an interest rate of 6%, the total value of the home would be consumed by interest in approximately 15 years. Because of this, most financial institutions cap the percentage you can borrow against your home to ensure that by the time you pass away, end the term or sell, the home's value is sufficient to cover the principal and accumulated interest. If you're not concerned about leaving your house as a part of your estate, or are using the borrowed funds to gift estate assets early, then a reverse mortgage may be a viable option for you. However, regardless of your circumstances, consider your options carefully and ensure that you understand the terms and conditions of the financial institution and the product they're offering you. Often, a quick visit to your lawyer for Independent Legal Advice (ILA) can be of benefit in this area.

Clear title – A title to property, about which there is no dispute or uncertainty about ownership of the property. In this case, there would be no liens of interest against the property to secure debt.

Many investors choose to liquidate assets to "simplify" their life as they enter retirement. Downsizing your home, selling the cottage or boat, or even going down to one car can all have great implications for your cash flow and investible funds. If you have rental property, the income generated from this investment will of course continue regardless of your retirement; but you may wish to weigh the pros and cons of selling it to draw an income off its investible value.

Additionally, many find it stressful to go straight from full-time employment to full-time retirement, and find that a part-time job helps in the emotional transition as well as the income transition. Perhaps you might start the business you never had time for while earning employed income or embark upon a whole new career. Retirement is the end of one job, but the beginning of many possibilities.

6
Segregated Funds

"The superior man, when resting in safety, does not forget that danger may come. When in a state of security he does not forget the possibility of ruin. When all is Orderly, he does not forget that disorder may come. Thus his person is not endangered, and his States and all their clans are preserved."

-Confucius

When I wrote the first edition of this book, I had neglected to include any information about segregated funds. Since then I've come to realize that a lot people have never even heard of segregated funds or have questions as to exactly what a segregated fund, or "seg fund", is and how it differs from a mutual fund. Well, first off, let's look at how they're similar. Both segregated funds and mutual funds create pools of money made up from a large group of individual investors. Both are available to buy or sell on any business day at current market value, and both generate returns based on the performance of the individual investments held within their portfolios.

Where the difference lies, is primarily in their ownership. Segregated funds are owned by an insurance company, while mutual funds are owned by the investors themselves. What happens when you buy a segregated fund is that you're actually buying a contract called an IVIC (Individual Variable Insurance Contract) from the insurance company which offers the investor the opportunity to buy one or more segregated funds. The insurance company will then return premiums to the investor based on the value of the investments within the segregated fund.

Now mutual funds have been around for a lot longer than segregated funds. Seg funds have been in the Canadian marketplace for several decades, but only really started to gain favor in the 1990s. The options for investment in segregated funds are steadily increasing, but still nowhere near the scope of mutual funds.

So why buy segregated funds? Well, they do have some distinct advantages over mutual funds. Their chief benefit is that they have a principal guarantee at death or maturity. Now the percentage of these guarantees varies from company to company and segregated fund to segregated fund, but you can expect it to be between 75% and 100% of your original investment. The maturity guarantee occurs at 10 years after purchase, and essentially means that if you had purchased a segregated fund 10 years ago and the value of that fund had declined below that of the original principal, the insurance company would pay you either the market value of the fund or the maturity guaranteed value, whichever was greater. So if you had purchased a fund with a 100% of principal maturity benefit, you'd get back your principal. If you had purchased a fund with a 75% of principal maturity benefit, you would either get the market value of the fund or 75% of the original purchase depending which was greater. Hopefully, after 10 years, you would have more than 75% of your principal!

Depending on the company and product that you choose, many segregated funds offer an additional benefit of resetting the base line. What this means is that after a certain period of time that you've held the fund, you may be entitled to reset the guaranteed value of the fund. For example, perhaps a year ago you bought $10,000 of XYZ Seg fund and it's value had risen to $11,000 over the year that you've held it. Your insurance company may allow you to lock in this gain by resetting the principal guarantee of the fund at $11,000; so if your fund declines from this point onward, you would receive at least 75% to 100% of $11,000 as a death or maturity benefit depending on the product you've chosen. Now, be aware that every segregated fund provider maintains different parameters for their products. Some funds may automatically reset and some may have to be done manually. Also, enacting a reset on a fund may trigger an additional reset of the 10-year maturity date to 10 years from the latest reset. It should also be noted that reset dates can be days, months or years apart depending on the product or company that you choose, so it's very important to get the full story when buying segregated funds so that you can compare apples to apples. To sweeten the pot further, some companies have added a guaranteed growth component to their segregated funds, stating that regardless of market performance, they will reset the principal with an additional percentage increase every year to compensate for inflation or just to provide some growth. If you're planning on taking money out of your segregated funds prior to maturity or death, the guarantees don't apply to the portion you're withdrawing.

Estate Benefits and Creditor Protection

As mentioned earlier, the major advantage of segregated funds is their death benefit guarantee. Depending on the product purchased, your beneficiary can expect to receive anywhere from 75% to 100% or more of the initial purchase amount. This is obviously extremely useful for older investors that wish to participate in potential growth greater than that of GICs or annuities, but don't want to take on unnecessary risk.

However, there's more to segregated funds than just the guarantees. As these products are owned by the insurance company, they are protected from creditors under most circumstances. Insurance proceeds generally fall outside of bankruptcy legislation. Investors that own their own business or are concerned about today's litigious society can protect their life savings with segregated funds. That is not to say that if you are in the midst of a lawsuit, that you can throw all your money into a seg fund and avoid your creditors. If the courts determine that the purchase of a segregated fund was made as an attempt to shelter assets with full knowledge of a current or pending lawsuit, they will deem the funds unprotected and so may be available to your creditors.

Furthermore, in order for the funds held in the segregated contract to be eligible for creditor protection, a beneficiary must be named. If the named beneficiary is revocable, he must belong to a designated class of individual. In most provinces, this means that the beneficiary must be related to the annuitant.

Another benefit of segregated funds is the avoidance of probate fees. As these investments are insurance products with a named beneficiary, they fall outside of your Will and, as such, are not subject to probate. This also allows the seg fund investor to distribute his estate away from the possibility of public perusal that probate brings. For many people, this may be a huge benefit. The probate system makes public all of your financial affairs and the privacy allowed by naming a beneficiary and avoiding this process may be invaluable.

All this protection can be extremely comforting, but is it necessary? Segregated funds can generally be purchased up to age 90, so if you're looking for guarantees to protect the principal for your estate, then segregated funds are certainly a viable idea. Just be aware that if you purchase a segregated fund between the ages of 70 and 90, most seg fund providers use a matrix to determine what your exact death benefit will be based on the age of the purchaser and length of ownership. But what if you're not really worried about death, but are more concerned about market fluctuations over the next 10 years? The only time the market as a whole produced a net negative return over a 10 year period was between 1929 and 1939; otherwise known as the great depression. During those years, market data similar to the S&P 500 Index showed an average loss of 0.9% per year for a total 10 year loss of 8.6%. While history can certainly repeat itself, the conditions in the "dirty thirties" were extreme. Unemployment went as high as one third of the workforce, while Germany and Japan were flexing their military muscles.

There is, of course, a cost to the additional benefits of segregated funds, and that is a generally higher Management Expense Ratio (MER) than an equivalent mutual fund. Essentially, you can expect to add between 0.4% and 0.8% to the regular MER attributed to a particular fund. This added cost goes to offset the cost that the insurance company incurs in providing death a maturity guarantees.

Who Should Buy Them?

Almost anyone can buy a segregated fund, but who would it make the most sense for? Well, if you are a more mature investor, say 55 or older, segregated funds may make sense for the benefits of professional money management and the opportunity for growth coupled with the security of principal guarantees at death or maturity. Also, as a mature investor, you may appreciate the ability of segregated funds to avoid probate while transferring assets to the next generation in a more timely and efficient manner. Segregated funds may also appeal to small business owners and self employed investors who want the added security of creditor protection. Finally, a seg fund buyer may be any investor who is simply averse to risk, but wants to participate in portfolio growth greater than that offered by GICs. These individuals may see the slightly higher MERs (and consequently slightly lower returns) as a small price to pay for the added comfort of the guarantees.

7
Tax Planning

"There's no need to fear the wind if your haystacks are tied down."
Irish Proverb

As far as I know, no one wants to give any more of their hard earned income to the government than they absolutely have to. As such, being aware of your personal tax position and how various decisions can impact you is extremely important. To date, the Canadian tax system is an incredibly complex entity based on progressive tax rates. That means the more you earn, the higher tax bracket you fall into. I'd like to point out here that tax evasion is illegal, however, the CCRA fully supports Canadians who reduce their tax bill as much as possible through legal means.

Before we get into the various tax strategies, you might need some clarification on some common tax terms. Marginal and effective tax rates can often be confusing.

Your marginal tax rate is the amount of tax you would pay on your next dollar earned, while the effective tax rate is the amount of tax paid once all income, credits and deductions have been applied. So if your marginal tax rate is 33% according to your tax bracket, you would pay 33 cents on the next dollar you earn. However, because of the progressive or tiered tax structure and any tax credits or deductions you may have, your effective tax rate may only be 27%.

Deductions from your paycheque are usually based on your projected marginal tax rate. It's after you calculate your effective tax rate, due to individual credits and deductions, that you are able to get money back on your tax return. So this example gives you six cents of those 33 cents you just paid, back on your tax return. Incidentally, the government doesn't pay interest on the taxes you overpaid during the course of the tax year. Your marginal tax rate is a blend of your federal and provincial taxes in all provinces except Quebec, where provincial tax is paid separately.

Types of Tax

Other basic but important information includes the three basic forms of taxable income. When most people think of income tax they envision the percentage of their specific tax bracket being applied to their earned income. This is accurate for earned income and interest income, but may not be applicable for income from other sources. For example, dividend income is subject to something called the dividend tax credit. The formula to calculate this tax includes grossing up the income generated, then applying a credit, with the net result being less tax paid than if the money had been generated through interest or earned income. Lower again is the capital gains tax. While many people attribute this tax to the buying and selling of stocks, it can be much simpler than that. For example, assume you bought a car for $10,000 and sold it for $20,000. The underlying increase in the net value of your asset is a capital gain of $10,000 and would be taxed as such. However, in the year 2000, the capital gains inclusion rate was lowered twice from 75% to 66% and then 50%, meaning that of the $10,000 capital gain earned on the car, only $5,000 of it is taxable at your current marginal tax rate.

Offset – Something that counterbalances or compensates.

The flip side of capital gains are capital losses. While no one likes to lose money on an investment, the silver lining here is that capital losses can be deducted from any capital gains you might have. It should be mentioned that capital losses can only be applied to **offset** capital gains and are non-applicable to any other form of income. As an added bonus, you can carry back your capital loss to offset capital gains in any of the *three* previous calendar years. If there are no applicable capital gains in those years, the capital loss may be carried forward indefinitely to offset future capital gains.

Borrowing to Invest

If you're interested in borrowing money to make an investment, the interest cost of the loan is generally fully deductible from your taxes. However, if you're using the borrowed funds to make RRSP contributions, the borrowing costs are *not* deductible. You can continue to deduct interest costs only for as long as you hold the investment that the funds were used to purchase. The specific investment held may change as long as all of the funds remain invested. It follows that when repaying debt obligations, always repay non-deductible debt before tax-deductible debt. To give you an idea why, you'd need to earn 12.7% on a non-registered (i.e., non-RRSP) investment to have the same impact to your net worth as paying off an equivalent amount of debt at 7%.

If you already have an investment portfolio as well as a mortgage, you may want to consider liquidating your portfolio to pay down your mortgage. Borrow again to repurchase your portfolio to create a deductible loan. Of course there may be capital gains generated by the liquidation of your portfolio, so speak to your accountant before such a move is completed. As well, *never* liquidate your RRSP portfolio as the funds will pass directly into your income and create a huge tax liability.

Income Splitting

In trying to limit the amount of tax you are required to pay, many look to some form of income splitting. Essentially, with income splitting you're trying to shift some of the income from a high income family member to a family member in a lower tax bracket. While acceptable to Canada Customs and Revenue Agency, certain rules can result in income being attributed back if done incorrectly.

Government benefits such as the Canada Pension Plan (CPP) payments can be split to lower your overall tax base. If your spouse has a lower income and subsequent tax rate, you may want to consider splitting your CPP benefits. For example, once you're both eligible to receive your CPP benefit, you can elect to split a portion based on the number of years you have been married or commonlaw. If only one spouse has worked and is receiving a pension then the splitting option becomes most beneficial. A side note on government plans is the $1,000 pension credit. If your sole source of pension income is the CPP and Old Age Security (OAS), you're able to draw $1,000 a year from your RRIF tax free.

We've covered a lot of information on RRSPs in our chapter dedicated to that topic, but there are a number of specific strategies you can use with them to further lower your tax bill. Should you and your spouse have incomes in different tax brackets, use the income from the lower earning spouse to make non-registered investments. The income generated off this investment will then be taxed in a lower tax bracket and the income from the higher earning spouse can be dedicated to paying household expenses. For your registered investments, a spousal RRSP may be the best option. In this scenario, the higher income spouse makes a spousal contribution to the lower income spouse's RRSP. A couple of notes of caution here: First of all, any withdrawals made from this plan before two years after the contribution, will result in the income being attributed back to the contributing spouse; also, the goal of a spousal RRSP is to create income streams that are approximately equal upon retirement, so don't just put all your money into the RRSP of the lower income earner without considering what each of your incomes will look like at retirement.

Other Retirement Tax Strategies

Contributions to your RRSP account always sound like a good idea, but cash is not the only way to do it. If you own qualifying investments you can transfer them directly into your RRSP and obtain a deduction based on the market value at time of transfer.

Don't forget that your RRSP contribution room has a $2,000 lifetime over-contribution buffer. This allows you to make an over-contribution to your plan of up to $2,000 without having to take it out or pay any penalty. If you go over that limit, you face a 1% tariff per month on the balance in excess of the over-contribution limit. Essentially this was set up to allow for accounting errors, but can be used to squeeze the very last drop of tax concessions out of the Canada Customs and Revenue Agency. Just be sure not to go over. One last thing about registered investments: Ensure that you've designated a **beneficiary**, or your entire portfolio may be taxed if liquidated as a part of your estate.

Beneficiary – Somebody who is entitled by a Will, trust, or insurance policy to receive money or property.

In making RRSP contributions annually, many Canadians receive money back after filing their taxes in April. While certainly getting money back from the government seems like a good thing on the surface, it is actually *your* money. This money has been sitting idle with the CCRA, while it could have been used for your own purposes during the year. So request that your Human Resources Department reduce the amount of tax withholdings from your paycheque. This affords you more available income to contribute regularly to RRSPs over the course of the year and may result in a greater overall increase to your net worth due to time in the market. Ideally, you'll want to shoot for a zero dollar balance (no tax owed, and none returned) at the end of next year's tax return.

Insurance & Taxation

While RRSPs are well known in Canada for their tax deferral traits, they're not the only way to beat the taxman. Certain exempt universal life insurance policies offer a tax-deferred investment component in addition to the obvious insurance benefit. There is no tax deduction for your premium payments, but as long as the investment earnings stay within the policy and the cash surrender value stays within allowable limits, they're exempt from taxation and compound over time much like RRSP investments. Similar to

RRSPs, you may want to structure withdrawals from this plan to coincide with a reduction in your marginal tax rate. However, if you leave your investments in your policy until death or attain the age of 100, the entire value of the policy, which includes both death benefits and accumulated savings, is paid out to your beneficiary tax free.

Medical & Charitable Deductions

Another quick tip is to optimize your medical expenses and charitable donation deductions. Medical expenses include dental work, prescriptions, equipment, transportation, meals, lodging, and more. By combining family medical expenses on one spouse's tax return you can generally get a better deduction than if you have claimed them separately. Expenses incurred in any twelve-month period on behalf of you, your spouse and any dependants can be used for the credit. Be sure to claim on the lower income spouse's return. For charitable donations on the other hand, combine them and claim them on the higher income spouse's tax return. Allow charitable donations to accumulate for five years before filing, as the donation credit is tiered. Have the higher income spouse claim the donations for maximum impact.

Investment counseling, portfolio management, and safety deposit boxes are also deductible expenses. Remember, you're able to re-file tax returns to correct missing deductions or credits generally up to *three years back.*

Income Attribution

Income on income can be a trifle confusing, but pays over time. Say you gifted $100,000 to your spouse, which he or she invested with a return of 10% or $10,000. This $10,000 is tax in the hands of the gifting spouse, but the recipient spouse is still free to reinvest it as well as the principal. Each year the gifting spouse would be taxed on the income earned from the gifted principal, but not from the reinvested income. Gradually, the income from this reinvesting income grows at a rate greater than the income from the principal due to the lower tax rate.

Offering to loan your spouse money at a special rate may sound like a strange proposition, but if executed properly it can be an effective strategy to save you some tax dollars. When you lend money to the lower-income spouse, you have to be sure to charge a rate of interest equal or greater than that prescribed by Canada Customs and Revenue Agency otherwise attribution rules may be applied. The higher income spouse must declare the interest earned on the loan but this interest should be less than the income earned by the investments of the lower income spouse. You must create a paper trail with this strategy if you want to avoid problems with Canada Customs and Revenue further down the line.

Self-employed Strategies

Self-employed individuals have a number of additional tax advantages. For example, as business income is not attributable, use a loan to your spouse to finance a business as the business income will not be taxed in the hands of the spouse who provided the loan. If you have a business, pay your spouse a salary for the work he or she performs. Keep in mind that the amount paid must be reasonable relative to the work performed. This spreads out your income to a lower tax bracket and allows your spouse to gain RRSP contribution room if they're not otherwise employed.

Tax Shelters

The old concept of tax shelters is a term that has all but disappeared. Some of this may merely be due to terminology. A tax shelter can be any investment that provides significant deductions against your taxable income. However, if you are interested in purchasing a tax shelter investment, do so on the basis of the underlying value of the investment itself, not just the available tax deduction.

To determine the quality of a tax shelter, assess both risk and cash flow after the deductions have been taken.

Flow-through Shares – Are shares of a corporation issued to an investor, who provides funds for the corporation, usually a Canadian resource corporation, for exploration or development work. Tax deductions generated by the work or acquisition are flowed through to the investor and deducted from the investor's income.

Most tax shelters are set up either as a limited partnership or as **flow-through shares**. Investing in a limited partnership essentially makes you a business partner and, as such, only your investment principal is at risk. Contrast this with flow-through shares, which allow you to claim expenses incurred by resource companies. These expenses also reduce your cost base and may result in a negative cost base, at which point a capital gain has to be realized to bring the cost base back up to zero. Tax sheltered investments have a much more limited market for resale, so liquidity should not be a prerequisite for owning these investments.

Alternate Minimum Tax

Excessive tax deductions can leave investors open to the Alternate Minimum Tax (AMT), which is specifically set up to target high income individuals with significant write-offs. If you aren't sure if the AMT applies to you, you need to calculate your taxes with the regular method. Then re-calculate using the AMT formula. You may want your accountant to do this, as the formula is quite complex. If the AMT taxes are greater than the tax owing for the regular calculation, then the difference between the two is the AMT amount payable in that year. If you are subject to the minimum tax, the excess of minimum tax over the regular tax payable is identified as a minimum tax carryover. This carryover can be carried forward for seven years and credited against tax payable in future years to the extent that regular tax exceeds the minimum tax calculation.

Holding Companies

Holding companies were once a staple of the affluent investor. However, recent tax legislation and substantial set-up costs have made them distinctly less attractive. Because of integration, a tax concept that dictates income earned through a holding company that distributes to a shareholder is taxed at the same combined rates as if the individual earned it directly, an individual generally receives the same after tax income on investments within or without a holding company. The net effect is that using a holding company may be more costly than beneficial and defeat the purpose of creating it. A possible exception may be found in using a holding company to save on the U.S. estate tax.

The Taxation of Mutual Funds

If you're holding mutual funds within your RRSP or RRIF account, the tax treatment these funds receive may not be of great interest to you because all income drawn from registered plans is taxed at your current marginal tax rate. However, if you have non-registered mutual funds, you may be curious to know why you had to pay tax on them, *even when they lost money*. As you know from previous discussions, mutual funds earn dividends and income from their underlying investments. The funds also create capital gains and losses when they sell these underlying investments. When this occurs, the fund distributes the interest, dividends or capital gains to their unit holders. Depending on what you've elected at purchase, these distributions may either be paid out to a cash account, like a bank account, or reinvested in additional fund units. Interest income is usually distributed monthly in money market funds and quarterly in other funds, and is recorded on your T3 Supplemental. Dividends are, of course, subject to the dividend tax credit and are made on a quarterly or annual basis. Capital gains are currently taxed at a 50% inclusion rate, which means that only half of the capital gain earned by the fund is subject to your marginal tax rate upon distribution.

Net capital gains, if applicable, are usually distributed in December. Foreign income must be reported on your tax return, but may be subject to a foreign tax credit for taxes already paid to foreign governments. This is summarized on your T3 Supplemental.

Returns of Capital can be a little complicated. For example, if your fund has a stated objective to pay out a regular distribution, but fails to generate sufficient income to do so, a portion of that distribution may be made up out of your investment capital. While this capital is not immediately taxable, it reduces the adjusted cost base of the units held, resulting in a higher capital gain or smaller capital loss on subsequent redemptions.

So the million dollar question is how, given all that information, does my mutual fund lose unit value and still cause me to pay tax? The key here is **unrealized capital losses**.

Unrealized Capital Losses – Capital losses on an investment that have not been crystallized by sale or a deemed disposition.

Imagine you were a fund manager who bought a stock that gained during the period you held it. You sold this stock and realized a capital gain. However, the next stock you purchase falls sharply after you bought it, but you want to hang on to it until the end of the year. This has resulted in the net asset value, or unit value, of your fund falling for the year. However, the unit holders of the fund still have to pay capital gains on the sale of the first stock you bought, as it was realized by its sale before you bought the second stock. The capital loss of the second stock has not been realized because you haven't sold it; so there is no capital loss to offset the earlier gain. Now, if you sell the second stock at a loss next year, that loss will be realized and may be utilized to offset any capital gains the fund makes in that year. Or, if the stock bounces back next year and you sell at a gain, the net asset value of the fund will have bounced back as well.

A tip for avoiding taxes in mutual funds: As a fund holder, if you want to get rid of what you perceive to be an under performing fund, you'll want to do so before December 31st. You may be able to use the capital loss to offset any capital gain realized on other investments during the year and reduce your taxes. The neat thing about capital losses is that you can also use them to reduce capital gains in the three preceding years, or carry them forward for future capital gains over an indefinite period of time.

If you're considering purchasing a fund that has a buy and hold strategy, you may want to investigate when the fund usually makes its distributions and ensure you understand its objectives. If a fund has been hanging on to securities for a long period of time, it may have large unrealized capital gains. Thus, purchasing this fund prior to selling these investments may leave you with a large unexpected taxable capital gain. This problem can become more apparent should you purchase funds late in the year. For example, if you purchase a fund just prior to its distribution, you'd be liable for the capital gain earned before you bought the fund, without having enjoyed the growth associated with it. So it may be in your best interest to wait for the year-end distribution, before purchasing funds.

8
Estate Planning

"Life can only be understood backward. Unfortunately it has to be lived forward." Arthur Schopenhauer

A common myth is that only the wealthy need worry about estate planning, and because of this Canadians often end up incurring significant and unnecessary costs to their estate and additional burdens for their survivors. Regardless of the size of your estate, planning ahead can reduce taxes and other expenses as well as simplify the process of changing the ownership of estate assets. My goal here is not to give you specifics on your estate, as provincial rules vary widely on the subject; but rather to outline a framework to help you decide what's important to you. Once you have a rough idea of your needs and desires in planning your estate, discuss it with a lawyer and accountant, preferably those with experience in the area of estate planning.

Before Preparing Your Estate Plan

Before plunging headlong into the writing of your Will, some preparation is necessary. Make a list of all assets and liabilities. If you've begun a financial plan already, you'll have this information in your net worth statement. Remember, even though you may know exactly where all of your assets lie, there is a large chance that your survivors will not (particularly if they're children). Quite often clients will have fixed assets and investments scattered all over the city, if not the country. If you don't want to itemize your assets in your Will, you may want to add an appendix, or even include with the asset and liabilities list the appropriate documents to be brought out at the necessary time. Having accomplished this, you now need to write out exactly what you'd like to see happen with your estate and what you'll have to do to achieve these objectives. Be very specific. No one can ask you for clarification when you're gone.

intestate – (latin) Not having made a legally valid will.

Naturally, the first thing you'll want to establish is who the beneficiaries of your estate will be. Primary beneficiaries may be obvious; your spouse and children are most often the primary beneficiaries of an estate. However there can, and should, be secondary beneficiaries listed as well. Secondary beneficiaries are named in response to the worst-case scenario where you and your immediate beneficiaries are all killed at the same time. Failing to include secondary beneficiaries may render the estate **intestate**, which leaves the distribution of assets up to the various rules applied by the province in which you live, and may conflict drastically with your wishes.

Having determined the beneficiaries, some consideration must be made about the impact on your family. Obviously this can be a very touchy subject, as often the beneficiaries either don't want to talk about it or hotly debate the scope of the decisions you've made. Regardless of the short-term discomfort, I've found that talking out your decisions with your family goes a long way to reducing animosity and ensuring that your intentions are clearly understood and carried out. Through your Will, you might also wish to address issues such as continued family support or the continuation of significant family assets.

When you've discussed this fully with all parties involved, then you're ready to visit the appropriate professionals to implement your estate plan. Depending on the complexity of your estate plan, you may require the assistance of a lawyer or notary, accountant, financial planner and possibly a trust officer. Remember, just like any aspect of financial planning, an estate plan is dynamic and should be reviewed periodically or at the time of a major life event to keep it current.

Your Will

Your Will represents the foundation of your estate plan, and is essential for ensuring that your wishes are carried out. A Will is a legal document that can be changed and updated at any time and only comes into effect on your death. Though most view the Will as a vehicle for property distribution, a Will also names an executor or executrix who acts on your behalf to carry out your wishes. The powers given to the executor may be limited by the Will or given greater scope depending on your wishes. There are two basic types of Wills; formal and holographic.

Formal Wills are typed documents created and signed in the presence of two witnesses. They're normally made by a lawyer or notary specifically because of their expertise in the area. A Will created by a lawyer or notary is designed to cover all of the necessary aspects of your wishes and objectives. While there are many Will kits available either on-line or in stores, it should be noted that these documents are generally not tailored to your specific objectives and may lead to ambiguity as to your intention in a specific matter. Should your estate be contested, the more specific the information included in your Will, the greater the likelihood that it will stand up in court.

A holographic Will on the other hand, is a document written in your own handwriting and signed by you. While most provinces recognize this type of Will as valid, it becomes open to contestability and is generally **not** recommended.

Regardless of the type of Will you choose, you'll want to review it periodically to ensure that it's up to date. The rule of thumb is five years, but any time you have a life changing event, or merely wish to change the instructions in the Will, you should have it amended. For instance, if you have another child and your Will is specific to only the previous children, your Will should be changed. Remember, if you're not here, no one can say for certain, or with any legality, what you really wanted to do. I wish to emphasize that Will amendments after divorce are *extremely* important.

Currently in Canada, almost 40% of marriages end in divorce which is, of course, a large change in your personal circumstances. In the heat of the moment and with many other things demanding your attention, it's fairly easy to put a Will amendment on the back burner. However, take the time to consider what may happen to your estate should you die after a divorce but before you're able to amend your Will. Certainly, the Wills Act may nullify gifts and powers as declared in the Will, however assets may go to an individual(s) you have no intention of supporting. Of course, the intent of the Will may be challenged but, given the cost, even if your family wins, it's just not worth it. The simple answer is to modify your Will as quickly as possible after a divorce.

Also provided in the Will, should be burial wishes as well as formal direction for guardianship of any minor children. Of course you'll want to discuss child custody with the people you may be considering prior to actually writing them into the Will.

Probate

Probate – The legal certification of the validity of a Will.

When an individual dies, the executor of the estate is usually required (depending on the assets under the Will) to file for **probate** with the Provincial Court, which requires the submission of the Will and a listing of all of the deceased's assets. This is done for several reasons, the first of which is to ensure that the Will is valid and that there are no other conflicting Wills in place elsewhere. Also, it formally appoints the executor of the estate. The probate fee or tax is determined by the total value of the assets that flow through the Will and varies from province to province.

A lot of people seem to get caught up in trying to reduce probate fees when planning their estate. While the reduction of probate is certainly beneficial, it shouldn't be pursued to the extent that it overly complicates your estate or runs contrary to the intent of your Will. There may also be unintended tax implications that arise when trying to avoid probate, resulting in a loss that may outweigh the gain you had hoped to achieve. Generally, taxes account for a larger portion of estate expenses than the costs associated with probate, so more emphasis should be placed on their reduction. The use of joint ownership can definitely help reduce taxes on the final income tax return, but may create a tax liability at the time of switching ownership, as well as the loss of control once ownership has changed.

Joint Ownership

Joint ownership is by far the most popular approach to changing ownership in use for estate planning. There are significant benefits to be had in joint ownership, however I try to make sure my clients understand the pitfalls as well. First of all, there are actually two forms of joint asset holdings. The first, and most often thought of with regard to joint holdings, is Joint Tenancy With Right Of Survivorship (JTWROS), which I'll just call joint tenancy from here on in. The second is Tenancy in Common.

Joint tenancy is a form of asset ownership that allows two or more people to share in full ownership, as well as control, of an asset. In this form of ownership each owner has equal rights to the property in question and there can be no proportional ownership (e.g., one person can't own just 10%). Upon the death of one owner there is no

Fair Market Value – A price for something that an independent third party could reasonably expect to pay in a free and open market when neither party is under any undue pressure to complete the transaction.

Deemed Disposition – Canada Customs and Revenue may, with regard to a transfer in the ownership of property, deem that it has been disposed of, or sold, at fair market value, and create a taxable gain or loss.

actual transfer of the asset, as the remaining tenants already have full ownership. Rather, the surviving tenants retain their ownership, while the ownership of the deceased tenant dissolves. As this occurs outside of estate processing, there are no probate fees associated with the asset in question. While this can be extremely helpful in estate planning and avoiding probate, there are some complications that can arise.

As mentioned previously, there is no division of interest in the property so a tenant can stand to gain far more than their fair share. This becomes more relevant in the case where estates pass to children. For example, if a Will stipulates equal division of all assets while a joint asset passes into sole ownership of one of the children a situation arises that may run contrary to the intention of equal division. For example, consider if you place the family home in joint tenancy with your oldest child to get around probate fees. Aside from the tax consequences, what if your Will specifically named all of your children as beneficiaries to your home? As the house falls outside of the Will (avoiding probate) it is not beholden to its intent. As such, the oldest child can keep the house all for him or herself and a legal battle ensues.

Another risk may be that if you enter into joint tenancy with your child and he or she were to become bankrupt, your property may be attacked to settle your child's creditors. There is a large loss of control with joint tenancy, as the financial interests of the group can be affected by the problems of each individual tenant. The deceased cannot control the use or disposition of a joint asset once he or she has died, regardless of what's written in the Will.

Finally, changing the ownership of property may result in tax implications. Going from sole owner to joint suggests that you have sold an equal portion of your asset to the other tenants and may result in a tax liability if this artificial sale results in a capital gain. This is referred to as a **deemed disposition**. The Income Tax Act recognizes transfers of assets by tenancy to be done at **fair market value**, so the Canada Customs and Revenue Agency will not be fooled by saying you sold it to the other tenants for a dollar and hope to avoid tax implications. Transfers between spouses, however, may be done at cost and trigger no deemed disposition.

Tenancy in common on the other hand is still joint ownership, but the rules are very different from those of joint tenancy. Two or more individuals may hold ownership, but there is no right of survivorship over the other tenant's portion of the asset. In fact, the interest you hold in an asset is directly proportional to the amount you put forth relative to the other tenants when the asset was acquired.

For example, let's say you wanted to buy an expensive boat, but couldn't afford it by yourself. Your brother decides to team up with you and you each pay half. In this transaction you may want to be tenants in common so that if one of you were to die, only 50% of the boat would be distributed through your Will (i.e., equal to the proportion paid for). Selling the boat would require the cooperation of both siblings. On the passing of a tenant, his or her interest in the asset passes on as per instructions found in the deceased's Will and, as such, is subject to provincial probate fees. This differs greatly from joint tenancy, as assets under that form of ownership pass outside the Will. If no Will is in place, provincial intestacy laws take over.

Intestate

So what happens if you were to die without a valid Will? If you do die intestate, your assets don't simply pass to your spouse or next of kin as many believe. Each province has different rules that define how much each of the estate's beneficiaries are to receive. Usually, the estate is divided among the spouse and children, with the spouse receiving the bulk of the estate outside of joint assets. However, having any of the estate transferring to the children before the death of your spouse may be contrary to your wishes. Also, most provinces do not recognize commonlaw relationships under intestacy laws and this may result in your commonlaw spouse being left out entirely. Without a Will your entire estate becomes subject to probate fees and a court appointed administrator would manage and distribute your estate. Unless a beneficiary is named in your RRSP or RRIF, the spousal rollover provision is eliminated, resulting in a greater tax liability. Also, legal fees may be greater and the court may appoint guardians for your children other than those you would have chosen.

Testamentary Trusts

> Trustee – Somebody who is given the legal authority to manage money or property on behalf of somebody else.

Trusts were once a staple of succession planning, but have fallen from favor of late due to restrictions in their use as a tax deferral or reduction strategy. However, trusts can still be an important aspect of your estate plan if used correctly and for the right reasons. Specifically, a testamentary trust can be set up to help control your estate on behalf of your beneficiaries after your death. In accordance with the details laid out in your Will, a testamentary trust only comes into effect upon your death. Assets named to the trust are held by the **trustee** and managed in accordance with the direction of your Will.

Trustees can have fairly limited or very broad discretion in the management of the trust, depending on guidelines laid out in the Will. The trust may be limited. For example, it may permit the trustee to only invest in the extremely short list of investments as laid out by the Provincial Trust Act. Whereas if specific provisions are defined in the Will, the trustee is able to invest the assets in a far broader array of investments. Regardless of the level of discretion, the trustee is still bound to act in the best interest of the beneficiaries at all times.

While no one can accurately predict when he or she will die, the timing of your death can have a huge impact on your estate. In the event of your premature demise, plans should be in place to control the risks of having your entire net worth fall on an individual or group who are unprepared for the responsibility of the processing, or the proceeds, of a large or complicated estate. One of the more important benefits of a testamentary trust is that in the case of minor beneficiaries, the trustee is able to provide the beneficiaries with support until they gain the age of majority or another predetermined age, without having to burden them with the responsibility of the bulk of your assets. I have three children, all of whom are minors, and I can't even fathom the problems that could arise out of having them instantly receive a large estate to dispose of at their discretion.

Testamentary trusts also provide an excellent opportunity for income splitting, as income generated within the trust is taxed separately from that of the beneficiary. Trusts can also be set up specifically to benefit adult beneficiaries who may appreciate the income splitting opportunity or may have personal complications such as a divorce proceeding or spendthrift habits. Children with disabilities can receive a lifetime allowance from the trust if that suits their needs. Spousal trusts can also be set up to provide benefit for the surviving spouse's lifetime, with remaining assets passing to the children upon the surviving spouse's death. This may be useful in blended marriages where you want to ensure your assets go to your children, but wish to provide for your spouse as well.

Insurance trusts can also be set up, where the proceeds from an insurance policy can be transferred to a trust. The use of a testamentary trust as the beneficiary of a life insurance policy may help avoid probate fees on your assets and offer income splitting as well as control over your assets after you die. If your spouse is currently the insurance policy's direct beneficiary, higher income tax costs may occur because the income earned on invested proceeds is added to your spouse's total taxable income. If a trust is set up as beneficiary, it can invest the insurance proceeds and all or part of the subsequent income can be taxed in the trust as a separate entity, splitting the income. Income that is directed to the trust's beneficiaries is taxed in their hands.

Living Trusts

The "living" or "family trust" can also be used as a form of estate planning, but differs somewhat from a testamentary trust. As with a testamentary trust, the living trust can be set up to provide long-term income and protection for beneficiaries, but as they are taxed at the *top marginal tax rate*, living trusts should generally not be considered merely for income splitting opportunities.

Gifting

Gifting is a practice that occurs constantly within family dynamics, but becomes more complicated as a form of estate planning. Parents often give small chunks of money or personal property to their children as they age and feel no ill effects from Canada Customs and Revenue Agency. However, if you intend to gift significant assets or stocks and bonds, you should talk to your accountant first. As with joint tenancy, you could trigger a "deemed disposition" and a "tax liability" if you're not careful. Also, there may be attribution rules applicable to the asset if gifted to a spouse or minor child for the purpose of investment.

> Gifting – If a person makes a gift of cash, assets, or property while they are alive, then the asset is not included in the probate fee calculation. If the gift is made to a child or spouse, attribution rules may be applied.

According to the Income Tax Act, income earned from gifted assets to these individuals is taxed as though in your hands. So if you give your son $10,000 and he invests this money in GICs, the interest that money earns is actually attached to your total income for the year, not your son's. The same holds true for dividend income. The exception to this rule is capital gains received by a minor child, as they're taxed in the child's hands. As with placing assets in joint ownership; gifting your assets represents a loss of control should you change your mind prior to your death.

Charitable Contributions

With government cutbacks becoming a fact of life across the country, charitable organizations are looking to personal and corporate investors to help keep their programs afloat. The government, perhaps with the hope of easing the loss of funding, has made it easier to donate by providing tax incentives for Canadians to do so. While many of us make small contributions to charities in one form or another throughout our lifetime, consideration of large gifts at the end of your life should be integrated into your estate plan. As with any aspect of financial planning, it is strongly recommended that you consult with professionals such as your lawyer, accountant and financial advisor before making any final decisions.

It should be noted that you don't have to give money to benefit from the Canada Customs and Revenue Agency (CCRA). Along with cash, tax consideration will be provided for assets such as stocks and bonds and rights to future payments like life insurance. Also, special consideration is given for cultural property, for example pieces of art or artifacts that represent our national heritage. Ecological gifts are donations of land to the Crown that may be ecologically sensitive and important to our national heritage.

Before making a donation, ensure that it is going to one of the 78,000 registered charities recognized by the CCRA. That being said, there are numerous worthy but unregistered charities operating in Canada and abroad, so you have to weigh the tax benefits of contributing to a registered charity over your personal preference for a charity that may not be able to provide tax receipts. When planning to make a large charitable contribution you must realize that it cannot be reversed once donated. Ensure that you will still be able to enjoy the type of lifestyle you desire for yourself and your family without the benefit of the funds or assets you're planning to pledge.

Depending on your province of residence, the donation you pledge may only cost you about half its face value. The federal tax credit is 29% and combined with a provincial tax credit of up to 19%, you may be able to get 48% of your money back. To make it even easier to donate, the CCRA lets spouses pool their donation receipts on one spouse's tax return. Generally, you'd want the higher income spouse to make the claim. Additionally, you can save up receipts for up to six years if you believe the annual donation receipts are not enough to make it worthwhile claiming them every year; especially since you get a higher tax credit on amounts over $200.

There is, however, a limit on claimable donations. You cannot exceed 75% of the net income reported on your tax return, with the exception of 100% for a donation of ecologically sensitive land or Canadian cultural property. Also, the 75% maximum increases to 100% for all donations in the year of death and the previous year. The excess can be carried forward for up to five years, but it expires upon death. As you might imagine, it may be more advantageous to spread charitable donations over several years to get the maximum tax benefit, rather than just maxing out in one year. Should you choose to establish a charitable trust, there is no limit to the amount of tax-free income that may be generated as long as it is paid to the charity.

Charitable giving should be specifically tailored to each individual. Factors to consider include your age, life expectancy and the amount of money needed to continue in the lifestyle you currently enjoy. Gifts of cash are most common and enable almost everyone to give to their favorite charity to a greater or lesser extent. Gifts of real assets, otherwise known as "gifts in kind" tend to be larger in value and less common than cash. Because of the diverse nature of gifts possible under this section, specific rules apply depending on the property donated. Be aware that the CCRA will not consider the full value of the gift for tax benefits if some form of compensation taints it, even if it's intangible (i.e., rights, privileges, advantages, etc.).

Gifts to charities can be especially valuable to people who face the prospect of passing away without a beneficiary to their estate. Rather than losing control of how your estate is utilized, plan to

Specific Bequests – A bequest made in the Will must be specific, and must indicate the amount, or the formula used to determine the amount of the gift. These details cannot be left to the decision of the executor.

make a bequest of your estate to however many charities you deem appropriate to ensure that your estate is used effectively. The tax credit your estate will receive will help in reducing the taxes paid, especially if you face the prospect of having large sums come out of a sheltered plan such as an RRSP or RRIF. If you feel that this is a course of action you may be interested in, be sure to give exact instructions naming specific charities in your Will.

Please remember that family members must be provided for according to law, and not even **specific bequests** in a Will can change that. In other words, even if you want all of your money to go to the 'Save the Iguana Foundation', you will be forced to provide sufficient financial support for your dependant family members regardless of the instructions in your Will.

An alternative to donating property or cash to a designated charity is the use of insurance. If you have an existing policy and decide to donate it to a charity, the cash surrender value of the policy is used in determining the amount of the contribution receipt. After that initial credit, any additional premiums paid on the policy will result in further tax receipts given to you by the charity. As you might imagine, the tax benefit you receive is limited to only the **cash surrender value** and **premiums**, not the actual death benefit the charity will receive on your death. This benefit passes outside of your estate, so no probate fees are payable. Alternatively, you may name the charity as beneficiary of the insurance policy while retaining ownership for yourself. This may allow you greater flexibility, in that you can always change the designated beneficiary should your personal circumstances change. The death benefit would result in a

Cash Surrender Value – Is the amount returned to the policy owner when a whole life insurance policy is cancelled. The cash surrender value is equal to the reserve value of the policy less any surrender charges.

Premiums – The sum of money paid, usually at regular intervals, for an insurance policy.

Living Trust – (inter vivos trust) A trust where assets are transferred into the trust while the settlor is alive. Taxed at the top tax rate.

charitable tax credit to assist in reducing the tax payable on your final tax return.

Those seeking immediate income tax relief may also be interested in “charitable remainder trusts”. In essence, you establish a **living trust** with cash or property, from which you draw an income for your lifetime. Upon your death, property or cash remaining in the trust is passed on to the charity. It can also be set up so that the remainder doesn’t pass to the charity until *both* spouses have passed away. As with any trust, there are pros and cons that may vary depending on the amount you wish to transfer, so consult your accountant and financial advisor before proceeding with this approach.

Some larger charities may have gift planners on staff, who will aid you in choosing a donation method that best suits your needs. On the other hand, smaller charities may not be set up to use some of the techniques mentioned in this chapter, so consult with your favorite charity before finalizing your charitable contributions.

Estate Tax

Many Canadians are under the impression that Canada Customs and Revenue Agency have created yet another tax, effective in the year of death, which increases an already heavy tax burden: The estate tax. In fact, the United States has a death tax, whereas here in Canada an individual is merely subject to a final income tax on their estate upon their passing. This doesn’t mean that their entire estate is taxed, merely that assets are deemed to have been disposed of as they pass on to their beneficiaries. Thus, all unrecognized capital gains or losses are crystallized, and net capital gain or loss is included in income.

Your primary residence is exempt from any capital gains tax, but any other property purchased that has accrued a capital gain is taxed on that gain. Also any interest or dividends earned by the liquidation of assets are included in your annual income for the year in which you pass away. This final tax return must be filed by the executor or executrix, and includes all income earned by the deceased up to the date of death. If the assets are left to your spouse, the Income Tax Act defers the deemed disposition to result in *no tax payable* until the spouse sells the asset or passes away. Don't forget, your primary residence is not taxable and may pass to your beneficiaries without any erosion of value.

Of all individual assets, RRSPs and RRIFs offer the greatest potential for taxes due upon death. These investments were exempt from income tax when they were contributed and sheltered from taxation throughout their lifetime, so any funds resulting from their deregistration *will be fully taxed at the individual's marginal tax rate*. However, if the RRSP or RRIF is left to the *surviving spouse or dependant minor child or grandchild*, the plan may be transferred *tax free*. In the case of dependant children, the registered funds must be used to purchase a 'term certain annuity' not to exceed the child's 18th year. Also, if the dependant child is infirm, the RRSP or RRIF can be transferred tax free to the child's own RRSP or RRIF. It should be noted that the Income Tax Act allows the executors of the estate, on behalf of the deceased, to make spousal RRSP contributions to the surviving spouse's RRSP account in the year of death or during the first 60 days following that year. This enables the deceased to claim a deduction for RRSP contributions on his or her final tax return.

Canadians who own United States sourced assets such as real estate, corporate stocks and certain bonds and government debt are required to pay U.S. estate tax based on the market value of their U.S. assets at death. Any assets that are considered U.S. situs property (i.e. located in the U.S.) will be subject to this tax. There are tax credits available to offset this additional tax, but it may be worth exploring your investment portfolio for specific U.S. property as you plan your estate.

9
Value of Financial Advice

"Success seems to be largely a matter of hanging on after others have let go." – William Feather

Despite the best of intentions, many of us invest more time planning our vacation or researching our new car purchase than sitting down and creating a plan for our finances. After reading or even skimming through this book, the process of organizing your finances may seem daunting. However, the fact that you've taken the time to read this book speaks volumes of your intention and/or need to begin the process.

The number of choices for investments is staggering. At the time of writing, there were over 4,400 different mutual funds available in Canada. Without even considering other investment choices such as GICs, Bonds, T-Bills, stocks, etc., this is a huge wealth of choice. With the advent of the internet, you no longer have to physically move from one financial institution to another to compare products; information is published for all to see and research. Narrowing down the variables would help immensely.

This is why researching and selecting a financial advisor may be one of the most important decisions you can make in planning for your financial health. A professional financial advisor has a strong background and extensive training in investment and financial planning, and is often equipped with comprehensive investment and planning software to help make structured recommendations and plans tailored to your particular needs.

As with investments, there are many types of financial advisors to choose from, so what should you look for? To begin, you can ask a friend or co-worker for a personal recommendation. Your accountant or lawyer may also be able to recommend someone with whom they have a professional working arrangement. Once a list of possible advisors is made, do a little research. What kind of accreditation does the individual have? In today's complex environment accreditation is very important and may restrict the kind of investments or advice an individual can offer. However, the advisor can have a wall covered with certificates and have no ability to relate to you or your needs. Your advisor can be in your life for quite a long time, so you'll need to be comfortable in their presence. How about experience? Experience is certainly an asset, but try to determine if the "experience in the field" is in financial planning or in a less applicable segment of the industry. Style is also an important aspect to be considered. Are you looking for a hands on advisor who wants to know about your personal interests and will keep in contact on a regular basis, or is it just the facts you're interested in? Compensation is an extremely hot topic these days. Advisors may be paid by salary, fees, bonuses, and commissions or any combination of the above. If an advisor is getting a commission, you need to find out if this is tied to any particular product or if it reflects an overall percentage of the business booked. Never be afraid to ask questions or speak your mind right from the outset. It's your money and, even if you're not paying fees directly, your advisor works for you.

Once you've narrowed down the field to a handful of advisors you might be interested in working with, you may wish to "shop" their services. Take in a copy of your most recent investment statements to each prospective advisor and ask them to analyze it for you. The key here is to treat each advisor separately. Get a feel for their style, level of service, experience and professionalism during the meeting. Once they've analyzed your portfolio, did they explain their findings to you in a manner which you were able to understand, or were they overly complex in their explanation? Did they highlight the pros as well as the cons in your current portfolio? Was the analysis just a cursory look or did they ask to schedule a follow-up meeting so they could give your investments the proper attention in the interim?

Once you have an analysis in hand, possibly the worst thing you can do is take the work of one advisor and show it to your current advisor or others you may be shopping. Given the opportunity, the others will inevitably say that they can do it better for whatever reason. It's in your best interest to ask each one to do their own work. Furthermore, they should not be made aware that there is more than one candidate in the running. If you really want to see how hard someone will work for you, give them the impression that there is no competition. A lazy advisor won't feel the need to put in a lot of effort if they think it's a slam dunk. With a few portfolio recommendations in hand, try to compare and contrast what each advisor has to offer. Did they listen to your comfort level with risk? Is the plan going to achieve your needs?

Another way to gain insight on an advisor is to attend a financial seminar. You can generally get a good idea of the advisor's style, focus and experience by watching how they conduct themselves in-front of a large group of people, and you'll inevitably learn something new. Most financial advisors put on regular seminars as a way of educating their clients and attracting new ones.

If you really want to be thorough, you can run a background check on your potential advisor. This may sound a little extreme but keep in mind, you are trusting this person with your life savings. It would be beneficial to know if this person's securities license has ever been suspended or if there have been client complaints leveled against him. Check out your provincial securities commission to ensure your new advisor has a clean slate.

On the other side of the coin, once you've chosen an advisor, be aware that they too have certain expectations of you. If you're going to trust your advisor to provide comprehensive advice on your financial situation, you must be willing to provide full and honest disclosure. It does no good to carefully implement a complex investment portfolio if the bulk of your investible assets are in undisclosed

GICs down the block at another institution. How can you expect your advisor to give you the best advice if he or she only has half the picture?

Now that you've completed this book, you may feel confident in your ability to manage your total financial situation, or you may feel overwhelmed by the complexity of choices and considerations - but at least you're aware of them. Having a broad understanding of investments and how to plan your finances will enhance the effectiveness of your relationship with your personal investment advisor. You can continue to use this book as a reference guide both to explain terms as well to trigger questions you may have of your investment professional. Starting with a foundation of basic knowledge of investment strategies, and building on this with a strong relationship with a trusted investment professional you should be well-positioned to make solid decisions that will positively affect your overall wealth. I'm not saying you should throw out the lottery tickets (it would be fun to be rich), but you'll no longer need to rely on a big windfall to fund your retirement.

Glossary

Annualized – To calculate or adjust figures so that they reflect a period of a year.

Attribution Rules – The attribution rules with respect to spouses provide that where property (including money) is transferred or loaned, directly or indirectly by you to your spouse, then all income or loss from the property, and any capital gain or loss on the disposition of the property will be attributed back to you.

Bear Market – A situation in a stock or commodity market in which stockholders are selling in anticipation of falling prices.

Beneficiary – Somebody who is entitled by a Will, trust, or insurance policy to receive money or property.

Cash Surrender Value – Is the amount returned to the policy owner when a whole life insurance policy is cancelled. The cash surrender value is equal to the reserve value of the policy less any surrender charges.

Clear title – A title to property, about which there is no dispute or uncertainty about ownership of the property. In this case, there would be no liens of interest against the property to secure debt.

Consolidation Loans – A loan for the purpose of consolidating all of one's debt in one product for lower interest rates and ease of re-payment.

Contribution Room – Anyone with earned income for RRSP purposes or certain other types of income can invest in RRSPs up to the end of the year they reach 69. Currently, the amount of contribution an individual has is determined by multiplying his or her earned income by 18% to a maximum of $14,500 (soon to increase) plus any room carried forward from previous years less the Pension Adjustment.

Deemed Disposition – Canada Customs and Revenue may, with regard to a transfer in the ownership of property, deem that it has been disposed of, or sold, at fair market value, and create a taxable gain or loss.

Derivative Securities – A security whose value is determined by the value of some other security or asset. An example of a derivative security would be an option or future.

Dividend Tax Credit – Refers to the preferential tax treatment granted to dividend income (common and preferred) received from taxable Canadian corporations. The dividend is grossed up by 25% and the tax credit of 13.33% is based on this amount.

Equity Market – An organized market where brokers meet to buy and sell stocks and shares.

Fair Market Value – A price for something that an independent third party could reasonably expect to pay in a free and open market when neither party is under any undue pressure to complete the transaction.

Fixed Trust – An unmanaged pool of debt securities that all mature at the same time. The pool is created by an investment dealer who then sells units of the pool to investors. Unlike a bond fund, a fixed trust has a limited life.

Flow-through Shares – Are shares of a corporation issued to an investor, who provides funds for the corporation, usually a Canadian resource corporation, for exploration or development work. Tax deductions generated by the work or acquisition are flowed through to the investor and deducted from the investor's income.

GICs – Guaranteed Investment Certificates are essentially interest bearing loans made to a bank or trust company for a specified term for a specified annual interest rate. Secure, because they are insured by the Canadian Deposit Insurance Corporation for up to $60,000.

Gifting – If a person makes a gift of cash, assets, or property while they are alive, then the asset is not included in the probate fee calculation. If the gift is made to a child or spouse, attribution rules may be applied.

intestate – (latin) Not having made a legally valid will.

Life or Fixed Term Annuities – An annuity that is paid out over a predetermined number of years up to age 90, or for a maximum of 20 years.

Living Trust – (inter vivos trust) A trust where assets are transferred into the trust while the settlor is alive. Taxed at the top tax rate.

Loads – A charge that is added to the price of some mutual fund shares as a commission or marketing cost.

Loss Leaders – An item sold at a price below its cost in the hope that customers who buy it will also buy other products.

Management Expense Ratios (MERs) – A calculation that is required under National Policy 39. It allows investors to compare the level of management fees and expenses from one fund to another.

Money Market Fund – These are considered to be the lowest risk of all mutual fund investments. The fund invests in money market securities, such as T-Bills and commercial paper.

No-loaded – A mutual fund that does not charge an additional fee, or load, is termed unloaded.

Non-Registered Investments – Investments held in accounts that are not included in a registered plan as recognized by the Canada Customs and Revenue Agency.

Offset – Something that counterbalances or compensates

Premiums – The sum of money paid, usually at regular intervals, for an insurance policy.

Probate – The legal certification of the validity of a Will.

Registered Investment – Investments held within an account, recognized by the Canada Customs and Revenue Agency, that defers paying income tax on the earnings of the account until the funds are redeemed or drawn from the plan.

Risk Tolerance – The financial and psychological readiness of an individual to bear the day-to-day fluctuations in the value of their investments. People who are unable to tolerate risk are said to be risk averse. Those who like to take risk are risk loving.

Specific Bequests – A bequest made in the Will must be specific, and must indicate the amount, or the formula used to determine the amount of the gift. These details cannot be left to the decision of the executor.

Trustee – Somebody who is given the legal authority to manage money or property on behalf of somebody else.

Unrealized Capital Losses – Capital losses on an investment that have not been crystallized by sale or a deemed disposition.

Vested – Having an unquestionable right to the possession of property or privilege. In this case, the pension contributions made by your employer are usually held to be non-vested until a specific period of time has passed, after which they become your property.

Volatility – Measures the periodic change in returns in relation to the average or mean return – the greater the change, the more volatile the investment. A volatile investment is a risky investment.

Deciphering the Acronyms

Pick up a financial advisor's business card these days and you'll generally see a string of letters after their name. Some you may be familiar with, but others you may not. In an effort to demystify the accreditation game, I'll give you an overview of each major designation.

CSC - Canadian Securities course: Administered by the Canadian Securities Institute, this isn't technically a designation though I see it on business cards all the time. It provides an introduction to investment products and financial markets and is generally the first step toward being registered to sell mutual funds, stocks, bonds, and other securities.

CPH - Conduct and Practices Handbook course: Also by the Canadian Securities Institute, the CPH is in essence an ethics course. It lays down the rules for the investment industry and councils advisors on how to run an ethical business and deal with various situations. Not a designation, but it may lead to one.

CIC - Canadian Insurance course: This Canadian Securities Institute course provides the information necessary to qualify for the LLQP or Life License Qualification Program exam. This course builds knowledge in the area of insurance and financial planning. Additional exams may be necessary depending on which province the advisor resides in.

PFP - Professional Financial Planning course: Administered by the Canadian Securities Institute, this course offers a broad based approach to financial planning and satisfies regulator requirements for financial advisors. It also qualifies advisors to write the CFP exam.

CFP - Certified Financial Planner designation: This designation is generally administered by the Financial Planners Standards Council and is widely regarded as the benchmark for financial planning qualifications in Canada.